10

D0905014

DATE DUE

Peace-On Not Leaving It to the Pacifists

EDITED BY
Gerald O. Pedersen

WITH CONTRIBUTIONS BY
William Lesher
Sigurd Lokken
Vernon L. Strempke
Otto Bremer
Ralph L. Moellering
Charles P. Lutz

AND A FOREWORD BY
GERHARD L. BELGUM

FORTRESS PRESS   Philadelphia

Inasmuch as it depends upon you,
live at peace with all men.

—Paul

Blessed are the peacemakers.

—Jesus

Biblical quotations from the Revised Standard Version of the Bible, copyrighted 1946 and 1952 by the Division of Christian Education of the National Council of the Churches of Christ in the United States of America, are used by permission.

Library of Congress Catalog Card Number 74–26328

ISBN 0–8006–1092–X

4662J74   Printed in U.S.A.   1–1092

Contents

Foreword: The Search For Peace

Gerhard L. Belgum

There is a stance appropriate to the Christian's search for peace. It is not that of a debater but that of a penitent, a faithful believer. For the search involves not so much argumentation as devotion, not so much persuasion as reverent openness—first to the Holy Spirit and then to one another. Christians today need to ask the question, "Do the Scriptures and the church have any significant word on peace for an embattled twentieth century?"

As Jesus affirmed with sadness, the issue won't go away; even with our best efforts "there will be wars and rumors of wars." Yet to recognize the connection between sin and endless conflict—even civil strife and global war —does *not* mean that we settle for combat as a way of life among peoples and nations. Neither does it mean that we abandon our neighbors in order to secure a private, spiritual, inner peace of our own. There are things we *can do*.

First, we can share with one another in Jesus' name. We can hear one another, and speak together in ways that were almost impossible a short time ago, when we were all hurting with different kinds of moral and spiritual injuries related to Vietnam. Once, we were so polarized that mutual respect and Christian love were smothered— on both sides of the ideological or theological fence. But now we can talk—and listen—even where disagreements may be really quite basic. We can declare a cessation of our own hostilities and defensiveness. We can get beyond emotion, beyond jargon, beyond the walls of our own personal fortresses. We can examine a variety of viewpoints and inquire about their Christian assumptions.

Of one other thing I am sure: we can consider seriously the Holy Scriptures. Too often we have been guilty of using the Bible as an arsenal of proof texts to hurl at those who are hurling other texts back at us. Now is the time to seek openly the whole counsel of God. To do so is not easy. It means listening for the paradoxes even in Jesus' own words: "Blessed are the peacemakers," and "I come to bring not peace, but a sword." When Jesus said "My kingdom is not of this world," was he advocating a monastic ideal? a pacifist ideal? a theocracy? an abandonment of all force, both physical and moral? a Christian ghetto? How do I reconcile the strenuous nonviolence of his Sermon on the Mount with his total opposition to evil and his verbal blasts against religious opponents? What does he mean when he says: "Peace I leave with you, my own peace I give you. I do not give it to you as the world does. Do not be worried and upset!"

When Christians attempt to "seek peace and pursue it" we have our work cut out for us, but we need not be worried and upset! Ours continues to be God's world, whatever we have usurped of it. And ours is Christ's church, even when we try to make it a reflector of our own opinions. Where the terms of the discussion are sometimes elusive, and even the goal ambiguous, the Christian stance is nonetheless clear: "Little children, love one another, as He loves you."

Preface: Seek Peace and Pursue It

Gerald O. Pedersen

In a recent message for the World Day of Peace Pope Paul made a fervent plea to all people to realize that peace depends on each individual person, and to be convinced, despite evidences to the contrary, that "peace is possible." Taking issue with what he called "an ancient fallacy" that proclaims man to be by nature aggressive and combative, the pope declared that modern people "must have the moral and prophetic courage to liberate themselves from this alleged 'inborn ferocity,' and rise to the awareness that peace is something essentially natural to people, that it is necessary, obligatory—and therefore, possible."[1]

With the United States having ended its direct military involvement in Vietnam, Christians in America have a unique opportunity to reevaluate their search for peace. The time is ripe for reconciliation, for reflection, and for articulating our vision of a peaceful world. What attitudes toward war and peace in today's world are consistent with the Scriptures and with Christian theology? What tasks lie ahead for the "peacemakers" of whom Jesus spoke? These are questions to be grappled with in the communities of faith.

Some basic assumptions of this book need to be spelled out:

1. Quoted from the *Catholic Voice,* 2 January 1974.

1) What we do here is done in the name of the Man of Peace. The gospel of Jesus Christ is our major resource for peace.

2) We look to the future and to the present, seeking constructive, positive, and realistic action toward peace. We are not interested in looking backward to be critical or to assess blame. We assume that all of us have shared in our past history and that all of us are capable of positive commitment to peace.

3) These chapters are intended for all—Republicans and Democrats, liberals and conservatives, reactionaries and radicals, "ins" and "outs," rich and poor, black and white, aged and youth, men and women—all whose central concern is to follow Christ.

4) We believe that the task of achieving peace on earth is exceedingly difficult, but that it *is* possible, and that we *can do* something to further the cause—in fact we are *called* to do it now.

This book has developed out of peace symposiums held in California at Pacific Lutheran Theological Seminary, Berkeley, and California Lutheran College, Thousand Oaks. Its purpose is to promote the creation of peace on earth as our response to the Prince of Peace, Jesus Christ, through awakening and informing the people of the church and activating them to follow the biblical injunction to "seek peace and pursue it" (1 Pet. 3:11; Ps. 34:14).

1. The Concept of Peace

William Lesher

"And when he drew near and saw the city he wept over it, saying, 'Would that even today you knew the things that make for peace!' "

—Luke 19:41-42

Students on our campus refer to the seminary as the Holy Hill. Its lofty elevation does afford a majestic view of San Francisco and the Bay Area below, one that evokes sentiments not unlike those Jesus must have experienced outside Jerusalem. Looking out over the fractures of life as he knew them to exist there in the holy city, Jesus wept. From the vantage point of our campus, or of your home, one can easily call to mind the multiple fractures that divide the lives of the people about us—the social, racial, and political cleavages—and to contemplate the suffering, destruction, and death these normal human fractures inflict. To behold the condition is to weep over it. And if the mind's eye travels out beyond the Golden Gate to points east it conjures up images of still deeper human fractures. Stories of starvation, predictions of mass famine, and questions about survival itself come rushing in like breakers on a peaceful shore. The view from Holy Hill can make you shudder. It can make your spirit weep for the world and all its children. Would that even today we knew the things that make for peace!

THE SCOPE OF THE TASK

Any serious grappling with the subject of peace must begin with some sense, some awareness, some recollection of the enormity and complexity of the topic. Yet this very awareness is in itself one of the obstacles to dealing with the subject. For the very enormity of the brokenness in our world and the very complexity of the structures that make for peace lead many people to withdraw from its pursuit saying, "There is no way, there is just no way."

People who take such a position share some prestigious company. John Hobbes, Karl Marx, Sigmund Freud, and a host of other thought-framers have seen little hope for peace on earth. They conclude instead that life is essentially irrational, consisting only of ceaseless struggle and endless conflict. Orthodox theology has followed a similar pessimistic route. Until recently at least, Western theology has been dominated by the themes of human hopelessness and human helplessness to do much of anything that might lead to peace.

It is not strange therefore that even today most people, including most Christian people, looking out over the brokenness in our world and contemplating the complexity of the problem of peace, simply turn away. The problem is too big, the fractures too deep, the subject itself overwhelming. The result, quite naturally, is apathy in the pursuit of peace.

We can all understand these feelings and attitudes. We all share them. But Christians are motivated by other feelings and attitudes as well. In spite of all the fractures we have an ancient mandate: "Seek peace and pursue it!" And we have a Lord who, having wept over Jerusalem, did not go home and isolate himself from the problem but went instead directly into the city and did many things.

He attacked one part of the system that was widening the fractures as he drove the rip-off artists out of the temple. He argued openly with those in the establishment about the meaning of authority. He signaled a new reign of justice and humanity by riding festively into town on an ass. He exposed himself. He risked everything—and he lost. Suffering and death may be part of the legacy for those who seek peace and pursue it as he did.

CHRISTIAN RESOURCES

Our faith in him, however, is our key resource as we pursue the cause of peace. There are understandings of peace that are unique to the Christian faith, and we will need to be well grounded in them if we are to pursue the task despite its complexity and the enormity of the present situation.

A Concept

Our first help relates to the concept of peace itself. From our biblical resources we bring a meaning to the word that stands in direct contrast to its general meaning in the English language. A quotation from *Time* magazine suggests the more conventional concept:

> Each week the 30-odd members of the U.S. Armed Forces Policy Council hear grim briefings from the Secretary of Defense and the Chairman of the Joint Chiefs of Staff on how much conflict there is in the world. Two weeks ago, there was a pleasant surprise. Admiral Thomas H. Moorer reported that as well as he could determine, during the week of Feb. 17 to 24 "virtually nobody is shooting at anybody anyplace." Moorer went on to declare that it was "more quiet around the world last week than at any time since I have been Chairman of the Joint Chiefs"—a period covering the last $3\frac{1}{2}$ years. It may have come from a perspective that only a military man could adopt whole-heartedly, but Moorer's assessment was bracing nonethe-

less. Said one aide, "He didn't mean there weren't some
people getting shot in Northern Ireland or that the shell-
ing of Phnom-Penh couldn't resume. But in organized
military operations, nothing was happening."[1]

At that point in time apparently nothing was happening.
There was no shooting. We were at peace. In English, as
well as in Latin and Greek, the concept of peace means
the absence of something, the end of something, the sub-
traction of something—shooting war for example. But
there is no positive full-bodied content to the concept
of peace. What do people *do* when they are at peace? Are
they dozing? Are they dreaming? Are they dead? The concept of peace as a contentless enmity inspires no great excitement. Many people have observed how, for some white
middle-aged males especially, World War II was the last
great excitement of their life. Peace is pale by comparison.

But we have a biblical concept of peace that is exactly
the opposite. It is full of content, full of life. The Old
Testament expresses it in the beautiful Hebrew word that
is gradually working its way into modern vocabularies
and dictionaries, the word *shalom*. Shalom does not mean
the absence of anything. Here the concept is not of idyllic
perfection but a vision of life fully lived. Shalom is a full-
bodied concept that includes vigor and vulgarity, compassion and conflict, all of life, fully experienced. Shalom
is something to work for. We never have it fully. It is
always becoming. It requires our best efforts, intellects,
and skills, individually and corporately. It is a total life-
style. One of the resources faith provides in our pursuit
of peace is thus a meaning for the term that makes the
search full and exciting, not a trip to a dull dead end.

1. *Time* magazine, 11 March 1974, p. 10.

A Vision

Our faith also contributes a vision of peace. Again, the vision contrasts with those of Hobbes, Marx, and Freud. It is a vision that peace is possible. Beyond that, peace is our origin, our aim, and our destiny. The Scriptures simply deny the cosmic pessimism of those who, because they see endless fracturing in life, consider brokenness to be our natural state and condemn humankind to a struggle of misery. At the beginning, the Scriptures hold up an image of Eden as original shalom. And at the other end, the prophets envision an existence where swords will be beaten into ploughshares, the lion will lie down with the lamb, and all tears will be wiped away. And in between the Bible sketches not a static vision of misery but a dynamic process of shalom breaking out here and there in the world. Isaiah 9:7—the prophecy of the Prince of Peace—posits the vision clearly: "Of the increase of his government and of peace there will be no end."

That's the vision with which our faith equips us. It's a vision that takes reality seriously, to be sure—we live in a fallen and fractured world. But this is not our true and only nature. Everything in us calls us to something more. We are made for peace. Shalom is our true nature. It is our goal. And here and there, now and then, it is also our experience.

An Experience

There is a third contribution of faith to our quest— from the faith we have an experience of peace. That's what faith is ultimately about. Jesus is our peace, and his peace is the basis of our peacemaking. Peter Berger relates peace to trust. He describes a child crying in the dark. The child's mother comes into the room and says simply, "It's all right" and the child quiets down and goes back to sleep. That trivial ordinary happening, so common in every home, has a cosmic significance! Because that's what we all want to know and experience—peace. We want to be able to trust something. When we can trust something deeply, we know peace.[2]

Christ and the cross are symbols of deep personal trust. Love and trust come clearest in suffering. Suffering makes trust worthy and it makes love credible. Christ's cross makes God's love credible. It is the cosmic word of peace. So we say that Christ is our peace. And it is the experience of Christ as peace that is finally the basis for all our peacemaking.

John MacQuarrie draws a distinction between the concept of peace and the techniques of peace.[3] With our vision of shalom we must address concretely the techniques of peace, the psychological, political, economic, and religious understandings and methods that can illumine and further the ongoing pursuit of shalom.

But it's a long search. And we will need every support to sustain us. Faith holds out a concept of peace that includes a meaning, a vision, and an experience to undergird us as we "seek peace and pursue it."

2. Peter Berger, *Rumor of Angels* (New York: Doubleday, 1969), pp. 68-69.

3. John MacQuarrie, *The Concept of Peace* (New York: Harper & Row, 1973), pp. 1-2.

2. Toward A Christian Position on Peace

Sigurd Lokken

A profound shift in attitude toward war has taken place in the American churches. The decade of the 1960s will be remembered by history as the time of vast and far-ranging changes in Christian thinking about the justifiability of war and individual participation in military activity. It was a change brought on by the ambiguities of American involvement in the war in Vietnam which continued on and on without reaching a decisive outcome.

It was a new kind of war in which we found that the old accommodations with aggressive hostility, under which we were used to operating, no longer worked. We were brought up short by a young generation who possessed a renewed idealism, and who, virtually in mass, refused to accept the traditional rationalizations for war. In one denomination after another, there was agonized reexploration of the church's tradition and movement toward a deeper questioning of mass violence in our time.

Underlying all this questioning and searching was a reluctance on the part of the churches in the United States to accept responsibility for the policies of the nation. It has always been too easy in the past to say that the burden of such fateful decisions falls upon others and that the church is a nonparticipant at this level of national affairs.

7

This attitude is fostered by the religious notion that the world is established and shaped for us by forces outside our control; all that Christians can do is make the best or most fitting response possible in a particular situation, the context itself being beyond their influence.

The task of constructing a theology of peace goes beyond this passive or "quietistic" stance to the point of accepting shared responsibility for the creation and development of our common life. Even Christians who say that the primary task of the church is to proclaim the gospel for all people must realize that such proclamation depends upon having a world with a requisite degree of stability and order. Hence, we cannot leave entirely to others the responsibility for governing this world in such a way that the gospel may have free access and that religion may be freely exercised so as to maximize human rights, justice, and peace. Martin Luther, the great reformer, stressed that Christians are citizens of both the kingdom of God and the kingdom of the world and, therefore, bear responsibility for acts of loving obedience in both realms.

OUR CHRISTIAN HERITAGE

Historically Christians have defended three major positions in relation to war: the holy war, the just-war theory, and pacifism. Of course, there are significant variations within each position, but the three categories cover the entire spectrum of possible choices.

The Holy War

This position justifies war on religious or ideological grounds as being absolutely right. God is seen as being on one side, and the devil as the adversary. There can be no negotiation or compromise, since one side is totally right and the enemy must be utterly destroyed.

While such thinking has seldom dominated in Christian history, it was the basis for recruiting soldiers for the Crusades during the Middle Ages. The holy-war mentality leads to a lack of discrimination about both the conduct and the goals of warfare. Any type of military tactic can be justified because of the corruptness of the enemy. The United States at least bordered on this type of thinking during World War II with its demand for unconditional surrender by its enemies. To achieve that goal, the use of saturation bombing and atomic weapons was portrayed as reasonable. Practical realism might better have aimed at a change in the enemy's behavior than at his total destruction and consequent submission.

The Just War

This theory can be traced back to the fourth century when Christianity became the established religion of the Roman Empire. It was used to justify wars against the barbarians invading the empire from the north. Augustine is generally regarded as the original source of this idea that war could be justified for the purpose of restraining sinful and wicked people who acted unjustly toward others. The theory went through much elaboration and refinement in succeeding centuries and has become the primary theological resource for mainline Christian churches in their thinking about war.

The churches deriving from the Reformation shared the Augustinian insight that Christians must share the responsibility for maintenance of justice, including the use of police force and military force. Hence, when Luther affirmed that it was permissible for soldiers to bear arms in a just war, he was voicing the teaching of the Catholic church in which he had been raised. On the surface, the criteria for judging whether or not a war is justifiable seem discriminating enough in themselves, given a sinful world where lawless people will attempt to gain advantage through the use of force. In contemplating war, it must be determined:

1) whether there is a just cause to be gained,

2) whether all other methods have been exhausted,

3) if properly constituted measures to declare war have been followed by a legitimate authority, and

4) if there is a reasonable prospect of a successful outcome—that the end condition will be better than the present.

Additionally, there are criteria regarding the manner in which the war is to be waged:

1) the conduct of the war must demonstrate a due proportion between the means used and the ends to be gained, avoiding unnecessary destruction,

2) the method of warfare must distinguish between combatants and noncombatants, protecting the civilian population, and

3) the goal of warfare should not require the utter humiliation of the defeated enemy, but mercy should be promised together with help in rebuilding the destruction caused by war.

The apparent reasonability of the just-war criteria is based on several assumptions. First, the existence of the nation-state as a sovereign, independent entity is taken for granted. European history in particular, however, reveals that national boundaries have been matters of dispute and conflict over long periods of time, thereby calling in question the ultimacy of national sovereignty. Second, it is assumed that the methods of warfare will be limited. War is seen as confined to the professional participants who determine the theater and the outcome of combat. Modern total warfare, however, with its vast range of available weaponry, can provide no protection for the noncombatant population and cannot therefore be compared with war in the Middle Ages. Third, the notion that military power can provide an ultimate solution for conflict between nations is assumed. But force may not be the final answer, for history is filled with the stories of people who refused to be governed by military strength alone. If law and order are to exist, there must be an optimum level of cooperation on the part of those who are governed. Without that, the aims of the conquering nation can be frustrated and defeated.

The terminology of the "just war" is itself misleading, for the several criteria actually have reference to what makes a war "justifiable." Indeed, for this reason some people prefer to speak of the "justifiable war" theory. A thorough study of the writings of those who developed and defended these criteria reveals that they never thought of war itself as either just or righteous. The actual combat, however "justifiable," must always be regarded as a tragic necessity, for which those responsible still bear the burden of guilt and sorrow for killing and destroying.

There are also difficulties in the application of the just-war theory. At what point are the conditions adequately fulfilled, so that the criteria in fact apply? The insistence that all other methods have been exhausted, for example, provides no help in judging whether those methods were truly as resourceful as possible and whether they were carried out with sincerity and good will. Certainly there are a myriad of possible relationships which can exist between nations prior to their reaching the level of suspicion, hostility, and treachery at which considerations of war are raised.

In cases involving civil war or armed revolution within a nation, the application of the just-war criteria is even more ambiguous. At what stage are injustice and oppression so inhuman that subjects are justified in attempting to overthrow their government? Citizens of the United States seem universally convinced today—as they were not two hundred years ago—that the revolution which brought their country into being was right and proper. At the same time, these same citizens are generally unable to sanction the struggles for freedom and independence that go on in our modern world. This stark contrast in attitude should lead thoughtful Americans at least to question this prevalent position. Such questions obviously will not be easy to solve; they will require the development of more explicit ethical criteria.

In spite of the several limitations of the just-war theory, many people believe that it may still serve a useful purpose as a guide to ethical reasoning about participation in war. It may be helpful to those who must make government policy and military decisions, to communities of Christians seeking to take a corporate position, and for individuals weighing their own decision about military participation. The Roman Catholic church and many Protestant churches have recently come out in support of "selective conscientious objection," that is, objection to particular wars as over against objection to all war. This position is dependent upon having the just-war criteria or some equivalent means to discriminate between wars.

Pacifism

This position undoubtedly represents the oldest tradition within the Christian family, and many would say it is the only justifiable one. Christianity came into existence as an intensely disliked minority sect in the Roman Empire. The early Christians were unquestionably pacifists, refusing to bear arms or engage in any form of violence. In fact, it was that basic commitment which made them distinct and set them apart from others. As we have mentioned earlier, it was only after the Roman Empire's acceptance of Christianity that the just-war and holy-war types of thinking developed. Expressions of pacifism can be found in every age of Christendom, but there has been a serious revival of the position in recent years. Once the exclusive province of the so-called peace churches, pacifism has spread to a wider base within Christianity and has enlisted support from nonreligious pacifism as well. This newer type may be described as "activistic pacifism" for, rather than merely seeking the avoidance of evil, it sees nonviolence as a politically effective instrument of social change.

It is a part of the shifting attitudes toward war that the mainline Christian churches today are seeking dialogue with the peace churches as never before. Just-war advocates and pacifists have been at odds in times past, both feeling that if their own position is right then the other's must be wrong. Just-war churches have sometimes found it difficult to support pacifists within their own ranks, even though these pacifistic church members stoutly defend churches' own teachings about the sanctity of the individual conscience informed by the word of God. Another impetus for the resurgence of pacifism in modern times has been the advent of nuclear warfare with the frightening specter which it raises for the whole of humankind.

A pacifist is one who opposes all war and armed hostility. The just-war theory which condones the use of war and violence under certain conditions is in conflict with pacifist commitments. Christian pacifism believes that it is a way of life based directly upon the life and message of Jesus: It is the attempt to apply the ethics of the Sermon on the Mount as if life on earth were in fact the kingdom of God. Pacifism does not regard itself as "passive," but rather as a form of peace*making* that deals *actively* with war and all other types of violence. Pacifists engage vigorously in the pursuit of justice following Jesus' way of life, nonviolence or antiviolence. They desire to be a part of society and to influence human affairs. They believe that society can be transformed by enhancing cooperation rather than coercion. The end of "peace on earth, good will among men" becomes also the means, and the means become the end.

Pacifists believe that Christians who hold to the just-war theory have not taken Jesus seriously, and that by condoning war they have contributed to violence as a means of solving individual and social problems. They feel that the obvious horrors of modern warfare ought to enable everyone to see clearly that pacifism is not only an achievable ideal but the most practical necessity of our time. If Christians cannot see that love is the greatest power in the world, then Jesus was a loser (as were Mahatma Gandhi and Martin Luther King, Jr.). Pacifists believe that their way of obedience make Jesus a winner. The failure to take seriously the message of Jesus and the "song of the angels" has contributed, directly and indirectly, to the extension of war and violence in our world.

The expanding dialogue with the peace churches is to be highly commended. If groups of Christians can get beyond mutual condemnation, there is much to be gained through the encounter. Certainly, we must all be one in terms of our goals, and dialogue can strengthen us in our mutual resolve. In particular, the mainline churches have much to learn regarding the strategies of nonviolence and nonresisting love.

STEPS IN BUILDING A THEOLOGY OF PEACE

A Christian theology of peace begins with the understanding that it is not sufficient simply to avoid harming our nation-neighbor; we must also seek his well being in all respects. We must become committed to waging peace just as aggressively as wars have been waged in the past. "He that would love life and see good days, . . . let him turn away from evil and do right; let him seek peace and pursue it" (1 Pet. 3:10,11).

The question has been raised as to whether a theology of peace is any more possible or necessary than a theology of boatbuilding, or cooking, or city administration; human efforts in all these areas, it is argued, are primarily matters of reason or common sense, doing whatever is sensible in a given situation. Our response to that question is that we already have a theology of war—the waging of war and individual participation in it have been elevated to sacred status with divine sanctions; we seek only the same status for those who would aggressively wage peace. In the churches it is those who would take action for peace who must justify themselves; the justification for war is already set forth—war is allowable if the specified conditions are met. Every effort toward peace, it seems, must first begin by justifying itself.

Therefore, we seek to go beyond the just-war theory. We seek to develop, if possible, more rigorous criteria than have been used until now, and to speak instead of a "just-peace" theory. An ethic based upon a just-peace theory will be more critical than before of military solutions to international conflict. It will be more suspicious of militarism as an ideology. Just suppose that the imagination, creativity, and resources now invested in the development of war machinery were invested in a comparable way on a commensurate scale in a Department of Peace. What might be the result? What is needed above all is a massive dedication to ending the use of violence as a means of settling conflict.

But even the ending of mass violence is not enough. There is more to peace than that. We need to come to a new understanding of what we are talking about when we use the word *peace*. As Christians, we are profoundly aware of how the Scriptures use the word—as a symbol of the work which Christ came into the world to achieve, and as the fulfillment of the intention of God for humankind. "Since we are justified by faith," says Paul, "we have peace with God through our Lord Jesus Christ" (Rom. 5:1).

The natural state of humanity, as portrayed in Scripture, is that of rebellion against God and alienation from other people. A person is afraid of God, distrustful and suspicious of neighbors, and unable to enter into harmonious relationship with either. The subjective experience of peace with God involves self-awareness and repentance, forgiveness and acceptance, so that fear of God is removed and replaced with love through the reconciling work of Christ. This new love brings about a consequent empowerment that enables people to come to peace with others: "He is our peace, who has made us both one, and has broken down the dividing wall of hostility, by abolishing in his flesh the law of commandments and ordinances, that he might create in himself one new man in place of the two, so making peace, and might reconcile us both to God in one body through the cross, thereby bringing the hostility to an end. And he came and preached peace to you who were far off and peace to those who were near; for through him we . . . have access in one Spirit to the Father" (Eph. 2:14-18). The wall of hostility to which Paul here refers is the ancient separation between Jews and Gentiles that has been overcome through Christ. The reconciliation of which he speaks involves the overcoming of all barriers and separations between people: "There is neither Jew nor Greek, there is neither slave nor free, there is neither male nor female; for you are all one in Christ Jesus" (Gal. 3:28).

Peace, in the context of an individual's relationship to God and to other people, is understood as the gift of God which he bestows when hearts love him and trust in him above all else. The gift removes fear, hostility, and self-protectiveness and conveys the capacity to love. Peace may be viewed as the result when other conditions have been fulfilled. When all causes of alienation have been removed, and when there are trust, freedom, justice, and safety, then there is also peace.

Peace is not static, however; it is not merely the description of a condition. Rather, it is the essence of a manner of relating which is the opposite of hostility. The dynamics of a relationship of peace make possible an entirely different set of transactions between persons or nations.

Peace may be viewed as an alternative means of coping with the situations of life, one that is different from the natural and the ordinary.

It is very clear how our Lord calls upon his followers to walk in the way of peace, to make peace, to practice nonviolence, and to use the tactics of nonresistant love. "Blessed are the peacemakers, for they shall be called sons of God" (Matt. 5:9). "Love your enemies and pray for those who persecute you, so that you may be sons of your Father who is in heaven. . . . For if you love those who love you, what reward have you?" (Matt. 5:44-46). "Do not resist one who is evil. But if any one strikes you on the right cheek, turn to him the other also; and if any one would sue you and take your coat, let him have your cloak as well; and if any one forces you to go one mile, go with him two miles. Give to him who begs from you, and do not refuse him who would borrow from you" (Matt. 5:39-42).

In the Sermon on the Mount, Jesus enunciates an ethic of a radical new kind, one that calls upon people to discard the ordinary, legalistic, and self-serving principles and to live confidently, generously, and grace-fully. This ethic does not ask what is right, or fair, or equal, but rather what is needed by my neighbors. What will be constructive and helpful for him? And amazingly, Jesus expects that there are and will be disciples able to live this new life. It requires a vision of what a world might be based on love instead of fear.

In general, church members today are able to accept the relevance of peace in regard to an individual's relationship with God. They further expect the church to be a place where that peace is experienced in the company of others who are "at peace." But, church members have more difficulty in affirming the church's concern for peace when it pertains to relationships among nations. This is perceived by many as a switch from religion to politics, from the business of the church to the business of government. In the main, Christians feel that their inclination is toward world peace, but that they have no peculiar or distinctive responsibility in this regard. The responsibility is shared with other good citizens; efforts at peacemaking, at achieving world peace, demand no more initiative from Christians than from anyone else.

However, it is plain that peace, political peace, is a part of the covenant of God with his people. The prophetic vision of peace in the Old Testament cannot be narrowly restricted to the individual in his relation to God and to the congregation of worshiping believers. To read those prophetic visions in the context of cruel and bloody wars on earth is to be struck with a winsome and poignant dream of the future that moves one to tears of deepest longing. "They shall beat their swords into plowshares, and their spears into pruning hooks; nation shall not lift up sword against nation, neither shall they learn war anymore" (Isa. 2:4). After portraying how previously hostile creatures of the animal kingdom shall lie down together, the prophet says, "They shall not hurt or destroy in all my holy mountain; for the earth shall be full of the knowledge of the Lord as the waters cover the sea" (Isa. 11:9). It is from Isaiah that we Christians have derived one name for our Lord, the Prince of Peace. About him the prophet wrote, "Of the increase of his government and of peace there will be no end" (Isa. 9:7).

Surely, it cannot be asserted that the peace we have been given through Christ has nothing to do with peace among all the peoples on earth. The task in mobilizing the church in support of world peace, of political peace, is to dramatize the religious and theological nature of world peace. This does not mean to depoliticize the issue of world peace, but to draw it into the realm of God's intention for humanity, and then to identify and organize the responsibility of humans in fulfilling God's intention.

Again, in this context, peace is not just a static condition. The cessation of violence, desirable as it is as a first goal, is not necessarily peace. We should be committed to that as a means of establishing the conditions in which peace can flourish. But peace itself will always be an ideal which is out ahead of human achievement, something that we will ever be trying to approach as love fulfills justice. Such peace can never be a "peace at any price," for it cannot be bought at the price of injustice and the continued suffering of the poor and oppressed.

In contrast to this view of the Scriptural picture of peace, some people absolutize the word of the first Gospel: "And you will hear of wars and rumors of wars; see that you are not alarmed; for this must take place, but the end is not yet. For nation will rise against nation, and kingdom against kingdom, and there will be famines and earthquakes in various places" (Matt. 24:6-7). They interpret this passage to mean that all efforts at making world peace are doomed to failure. But even if this were so, does that excuse us Christians from making the effort in every generation? Perhaps some of us have absolutized another theme in Scripture, "Blessed are the peacemakers . . . seek peace," yet there is ample justification for choosing this emphasis—God's will *is* peace!

The witness of young conscientious objectors has been an inspiration to many of us. In a very honest and human fashion they simply took the teachings of Jesus at face value and sought to live according to them. Theirs was a response that had not been put through the strainer of theological rationalism over the course of many centuries. At a very elementary and personal level, they simply said that they would not kill, that war is wrong. Why is it seemingly so difficult for Christians generally to accept that position?

THE CORPORATE RESPONSIBILITY OF CHRISTIANS

We are concerned, as peacemakers, not only to provide guidance for individuals facing moral choices about war, but also to foster a climate in which the church may corporately take a moral stance. Oftentimes to do so will not be popular; it may even be divisive within the church. Yet the capability of reaching such moral concensus is of utmost importance. In churches of the Reformation tradition there is tremendous respect for the rights of individual conscience, perhaps owing to Luther's own insistence, even before the emperor, that he could not go against conscience. The Protestant tradition values highly the power of the individual conscience to make responsible decisions in the light of the word of God. Such an emphasis necessarily leads to divergent forms of response under the guidance of the Holy Spirit. Legislation of any type and rules of moral behavior are carefully avoided.

This form of highly individualistic ethics can help solve some of the problems persons have in relation to society, but situations may also arise in which it is impossible to sanction just any decision whatever made by an individual in isolation, simply because that person made it. We will have to explore more deeply the way that conscience is formed and developed, for in our tradition we do not believe that individual conscience is a direct pipeline to God. Likewise, if we leave every important issue to the realm of individual decision, we lose our ability to lend the weight of our support to members being questioned or rebuked for their decisions.

The church must accept responsibility for the role it plays in guiding the development of an individual's conscience; it must also become a real community of support that can affirm that person in his stance. The question then becomes: What is the range of possible options that the church can support and still maintain that the individual member is a Christian operating within a Christian understanding of life? Even in the post-Vietnam era we still feel the agonies arising out of the ambiguities of American involvement in the Far East. The wounds caused by our differing opinions about national policy and action have not yet been healed, either in church or nation—and cannot be so long as those who could not conscientiously participate have not been offered amnesty and welcomed home.

The ability of the church to speak corporately is closely tied to its power to be an influence in government, and we have not yet faced much less mastered the problem of how to play a responsible role in modern democracy. In the situation today, so different from that of earlier eras, we are not only responsible *to* the governing authorities as in the days when the bishop gave his counsel to the king. In a twentieth-century democracy we are also a part of the government itself; both as individual Christians and as an institutional church we have a responsibility *for* governing.

The church in America often feels itself to be a powerless institution in society. This feeling may too easily lead us to abdicate our responsibility for the quality of our

common life. The church is potentially a powerful institution. However, it must still realize and actualize that
power. Its potential is not in the area of coercive force,
of course, but in the area of moral power. The capacity to
discern and tell what is good and right and true is still a
great power. King David was so convicted by the word
of a rural prophet that he changed the way he had been
acting. In a time when the popular tendency is to deify
the state so that it can do whatever it wills, then the
church can and must lift its voice to say that government
must never demand the allegiance due only to God.

THE NEED TO BUILD A SENSE OF WORLD COMMUNITY

There are many factors today which are causing us to
become increasingly aware of the world as a global community or, picturesquely, as "Spaceship Earth." Increased
world travel, instant global communications, ecological
concerns of planet-wide proportions, and awareness of our
ever-increasing dependence upon regional resources all
help us to see that we cannot live in isolation. "No man
is an island," nor is any nation an island in the sea of contemporary world affairs. In spite of occasional, sometimes high-level protestations about our need for
"independence" in energy resources, this field or that, our
experience is that of ever more obvious worldwide interdependence. It is more true today than ever before that as
a world "either we must learn to hang together, or we will
hang separately."

In short, the time is long overdue for the development
of a new sense of world community as over against the
old sense of the independence of the sovereign nation-
state. One can wonder how the notion of the absolute
power of individual nations has persisted so long. Yet,
nothing raises more fears or seems more threatening than

that there should come into being a power which would be above "my country." For this reason, the United Nations meets with only half-hearted acceptance, and is rejected out of hand by many citizens. When Romans 13 calls upon Christians to be subject to the governing authorities, how dare we limit those authorities to those of national scope and origin? In the divine plan, are not international structures aiming at order and stability also a valid part of those governing authorities.

Churches have a unique opportunity to assist in building world community through the international bonds and associations which already mark the Christian fellowship. The church, by its very nature, is not national but international and worldwide. National, racial, ethnic, and economic barriers which tend to keep people apart have often been overcome in the communion of the church. A shared religious faith and mission can help bring about an otherwise difficult transcultural acceptance. The Christian community should have resources within it to transcend the political or materialistic issues that are the source of international conflict.

Through the exchange of visitors, the sending of missionaries from as well as to the "developing" countries, and the provision of needed aid in emergency situations, a feeling of goodwill can be built that is conducive to international trust. In partnership with our fellow believers in every land, we Christians can commit ourselves to the task of building a community based upon the vision of a world at peace.

3.   Psychology and Peace

Vernon L. Strempke

Psychologists endeavor through study and experimentation to establish principles which explain, predict, and influence human thought and behavior. They desire to understand the total range of human experience, and to attempt explanations for people's motives, thoughts, and emotions. For many psychologists the phenomena of war and peace also come within the range of their interest and concern.

Psychology of course does not purport to provide any final answer or answers to the questions of our inquiry into the causes of war and the resources for peace. There can be no such answers to problems of such magnitude! Nevertheless, some increments of understanding regarding these concerns can be offered and have been offered. The complexity of the themes requires pooling of knowledge, collaborative effort, and better communication at various levels among representatives of all the various sciences, disciplines, policy-makers, practitioners, and the general public.

Our purpose here will be to identify and interpret certain psychologically significant characteristics of thought and conduct among Christians in respect to war and peace. We will focus more on the psychological causes of war than on the resources for peace because an understanding of the former necessarily has such important implications

for the latter—implications which are of special significance for Christians.

THE VIEW OF MAN AND THE EXPECTATIONS OF WAR

The views of man held by many Christians do not support confidence in or motivation for human efforts toward
peace. They make the injunction to "seek peace and pursue
it" (1 Pet. 3:11), a troublesome and discouraging
mandate.

Christians typically view man's nature in terms of its
perverseness or, worse, its depravity. Martin Luther, the
Protestant Reformer, often quoted Isaiah 64:6: "We are
all of us unclean, and all our righteousness is as a filthy
stinking rag."[1]

Christians tend to make negative assessments of themselves and of others, regularly confessing in their worship
the belief that "we are by nature sinful and unclean, and
that we have sinned against thee by thought, word and
deed."[2]

Luther was convinced by the Scriptures that there is
absolutely no innate good in man. Man possesses a pro-
pensity toward evil, which is the heritage of each individual by virtue of his human origin. The evil tendencies
of the self express themselves in actual or open violations
of the word of God and the rights of men.[3] According to
Luther, reason will not by itself lead man to an accurate,
scriptural evaluation of human nature. The impotence of

1. See, e.g., American Edition of Luther's Works (Philadelphia:
Fortress, and St. Louis: Concordia, 1955—) [hereinafter cited as
LW] 32, 83; cf. *LW* 21, 352.
2. *Service Book and Hymnal* (Philadelphia: United Lutheran
Church in America, 1958), p. 1.
3. *LW* 32, 29.

human reasoning only makes man blind to the helpless state in which he finds himself.[4]

Man's natural motivations are contrary to God. The human will, which in the opinion of Luther is synonymous with the ego, is in a state of bondage to the devil, the natural self, and sin. The ego's lack of freedom makes it utterly impossible for man to enter into an honorable relationship with God, at best the ego feebly assists man to confront the demands of his external world.[5]

Man did not and does not *necessarily* have to suffer his depraved state and its consequences, however. That was and is man's *choice*. The Reformers held that man was created in God's image and given a life of bliss but that man was simultaneously given the option of rejecting his "blessed state" by separating himself from God. This was in fact what man chose to do. By his "fall" man lost his original innocence and exchanged his state of bliss for one of sin and misery. Man's fundamental error was his refusal to put full trust and confidence in God and his word. This sinful tendency stems from the human self, which constantly seeks to exalt itself on the basis of a false evaluation of its own nature and works.

In his own theology Luther more than balanced his negative assessments of man's potential with an emphasis on the positive potentials through faithful obedience to Christ.[6]

The person who believes in Christ enters into a new life of victory over sin, self, and the devil. The trusting relationship with God generates in man new powers by which to control the ego or will as well as the conduct of daily

4. *LW* 39, 63.
5. *LW* 32, 92.
6. *LW* 31, 347.

life. The powers within the regenerated man propel him to ever higher levels of holiness in daily living which reflect the teachings of Jesus Christ.[7]

Though Christian views of man's nature express optimism regarding man's "justification by faith in Christ," this optimism, for Luther, is tempered by the countertheme of "simul justus et peccator": man is saint and sinner at one and the same time.[8]

This is interpreted by many Christians on the basis of instruction and experience, to mean that the outcome of the conflict between Christ and Satan over "body and soul" is precarious and doubtful. For many people the dynamic tension inherent in Luther's theological stance is less than assuring and satisfying. Its ambiguous, even schizophrenic, character leaves them with a sense of hopelessness and futility regarding man.

The resulting negativism regarding man helps make many Christians fatalistic, pessimistic, or at best perhaps, only apathetic with respect to war. They tend to regard war as inevitable. They often quote Jesus' words in support of this conclusion: "There will always be wars and rumors of war."[9]

Behavioral scientists who study the psychological issues involved in the nature of war are concerned about the widespread assumption that war is an inexorable consequence of man's nature and that all efforts to eliminate it are therefore doomed to failure.[10]

7. *LW* 41, 145-46.
8. *LW* 35, 376-77.
9. Matt. 24:6; Mark 13:7.
10. Group for the Advancement of Psychiatry, *Psychiatric Aspects of the Prevention of Nuclear War,* 104 E. 25th St., New York, N.Y. 10010, 1964; p. 229.

Psychologists are keenly aware of the considerable evidence which seems to support the commonly held hypothesis that war must be indigenous to human nature. Countless wars recorded in human history and abundant experiential data seem to confirm man's powerful tendencies toward violent, destructive behavior, and to justify the conclusion among the rank and file of people that it is the destructive behavior of individuals which makes possible collective expressions of aggressiveness and hostility in large scale warfare.

But on close inspection this theory, that wars are the sum total of countless individual human aggressions, is untenable, particularly when applied to contemporary situations of national and international conflict. Psychologists argue that, even if destructive aggression were indubitably an innate human instinct, it would not necessarily mean that war is inevitable.[11]

Modern warfare is a complicated institution; it is a product of many intermeshing factors—social, political, economic, religious, and psychological. A contemporary war of significant magnitude involves intricate planning, massive preparation, and huge expenditures of resources. It requires scientific technology, effective propaganda, and systematic recruitment of human and other resources. War is not something one man undertakes on his own, in consequence of his own hostile or aggressive feelings. Only after all complicated preparations for war have been accomplished and the wheels of the war machine are ready to turn, can one man indeed start a war. But even then the complexity of military maneuvers and the precision of their execution requires controlled, studied judgments on the part of many persons. These largely dispassionate ac-

11. Ibid.

tivities do not facilitate the direct expression of hatred and anger. It is a paradox of modern warfare, in contrast to the battles of primitive societies, that as technology has advanced, aggressive feelings per se have become progressively inconsequential. The push-button weaponry of our nuclear age requires calm, scientific precision—not passion—for their effective use. The destructive characteristics of man, therefore, can no longer be cited as the sole cause of war or the major frustration of efforts toward peace. They simply do not explain the institutional nature of war. Social institutions are deeply rooted in human nature, of course, but they do not necessarily have to produce violence and destruction. Furthermore, social institutions are potentially capable of evolution, change, and even eradication. For example, society has almost eliminated cannibalism, dueling, rites of human sacrifice, and slavery. History and anthropology document the existence of societies which have rarely—even never—experienced war. Therefore, the practice of war and its existence as a social institution cannot be explained solely in terms of man's hostile and aggressive nature.

Psychological Mechanisms Relating to War

Though a heavy emphasis on man's violent nature does not explain war, it does play an important psychological role in the acceptance of war. A negative view of man constitutes an important psychological barrier to efforts aimed at the elimination of war. For example, pacificism is rejected by many Christians as impractical idealism or even heresy because it denies the existence of original sin. Such opinions not only frustrate the quest for peace but also facilitate the mobilization of man's destructiveness in support of violent conflict.

The Acceptance of War

It has been argued that man's depravity not only makes war inevitable, but that its utilization toward that end is under certain circumstances right and proper. The exercise of man's destructiveness and violence are sanctioned for the good of the group. What might be considered wrong or immoral when done by the individual becomes, when sanctioned by the group, not only acceptable but totally proper and right, so right that omitting to do it is deemed wrong. An individual may not approve the killing of another person upon sight or provocation. However, in war such killing not only may be authorized but commanded.

The Stereotyping of the Enemy

A keen awareness of man's evil nature creates a "readiness to act"—in fact, can produce a defensive overreaction toward a stereotyped enemy. During wartime and in the process of mobilizing for war, "the enemy" is easily seen to manifest more of man's learned propensities toward evil than of any positive human potentials acquired in consequence of divine intervention. The overwhelming preoccupation with "what they might do to us" may be a projection of man's conditioned response to anxiety, fear, and hatred. It may result from the overpowering realization that "I, you, and we are evil." The violent expression of anxiety, depression, and hostility toward oneself and toward others for being "by nature sinful and unclean" could be cathartic and in some instances therapeutic. Such destructive "acting out" of feelings based on introjected evaluations of man's evil nature could be for some persons as emotionally satisfying as the receiving of forgiveness—or even more so! Even though persons are only peripherally involved in the violence, they could nevertheless thereby experience a vicarious release from their captivity under the judgment of being evil—"no good" like all mankind.

Killing Made Honorable

The psychological mechanisms of stereotyping, projecting, and introjecting help explain why Christians, like non-Christians, can often attribute to soldiers without qualification the "manly" virtues of heroism and courage for killing people and destroying property. In this connection it is worthwhile noting that most of the great popular heroes of history have been soldiers. When war is glorified as brave, just, righteous, and honorable, persons with Christian convictions could be sublimating their unacceptable feelings and thoughts about the evil in themselves and in the enemy. Since war can be an unconsciously desired cleansing for the individual or corporate self, we give corresponding praise to those who dare to achieve the most at the greatest risk.

Dehumanization Through Passive Obedience

Authority is a problem for many people and in this respect Christians are no exception. With Romans 13 as a scriptural basis, Christians have obeyed governmental authority and interpreted such obedience as loyalty and patriotism. Even in situations of social abuse and political tyranny they have accepted Paul's counsel, "Let every soul be subject unto the higher powers . . . the powers that be are ordained of God" (Rom. 13:1).

Though Christians may be obedient to governmental authority, they aren't all blind to its evils. Most Christians grant conditional authority to government, which means that government is capable of error and is afflicted with evil. They are critical but in a passive style. Any overt gesture against the government creates anxiety and disturbs their preferred silent acquiescence. The highest patriotism or loyalty for them is blind acceptance rather than aggressive involvement in vigorous debate, constructive criticism, or legislative reform. These are the Christians who do not major in social, political, or legislative action. They allow others to assume leadership and responsibility for these areas of civic involvement.

When the passive obedience of some Christians toward authority is considered psychologically, masochistic tendencies toward self-dehumanization can be identified. As people inhibit, repress, and disguise their true opinions and emotions, they alter their self-image. In defending themselves from human feelings and states of mind, they compartmentalize their emotions and pauperize their capacities for feeling and acting like human beings. The danger of alteration of self-image and dehumanization can be seen in reactions such as these: "I am only following orders," "They (the government, the people in authority) probably know what they are doing," "Who am I to question that? What good would it do for me to say something?" Such responses create a self-image devoid of the qualities of courage, power, autonomy, confidence, and responsibility which are usually identified with a healthy self-image.

Though every person confronts dehumanization to some degree in many relationships and transactions, nevertheless, when this destructive process prevents people from maintaining a predominant state of well-being, it is harmful or maladaptive. The more real the need or justification for adaptively using the process of dehumanization, the easier it is to miss the transition point where the intended ego-supportive device becomes destructive—to others as well as to self. If a person as a potential voter can't read English, the privilege of voting in some instances must be forfeited. This would be an adaptive but dehumanizing adjustment to the inability to read English. The dehumanizing process of adjustment would be maladaptive in the event such a person withdrew from society and lived as a recluse.

Because they are immigrants—or offspring of immigrants—some ethnic Christians in the United States have had feelings of being alien, inferior, or inadequate. Many came to this country for the purpose of escaping military conscription, economic deprivation, and social estrangement. For most of these the escape was successful, except for the consequential dehumanizing impact upon their self-image. This dehumanization was felt in terms of inferiority, inadequacy, even helplessness. During World Wars I and II these feelings became pronounced among many whose alien ancestry was obvious by virtue of their language, name, or other identifying characteristics. As a result the dehumanization contributed to anxiety, timidity, indifference, passivity, or in some instances compensational aggressiveness. Such responses, for example, were evident in reactions to governmental policies of commitment to war, and in the absence of influential guilt feelings over behavior which dehumanizes others, for example, mass murder by bombing. Among some Christians this dehumanization process may even contribute today to a denial of responsibility for current efforts toward peace.

In summary, the following psychologically significant observations have been identified which influence the attitudes and behavior of many Christians regarding war:

1) The heavy emphasis on man's sinful nature leads some Christians to regard peace as impossible and peace efforts as futile.

2) The pervasive awareness of man's evil nature creates a readiness to act and overreact toward a stereotyped, depraved enemy inside and outside self.

3) The individual's unacceptance of self, in fact, his or her self-hate can be expressed cathartically through hostile or aggressive behavior; such behavior may be compensatory; even though it may lead to the destruction of human life it can be considered brave, heroic, and noble.

4) Attitudes among some Christians toward authority have encouraged unhealthy self-images and processes of masochism and dehumanization.

At issue in all of this is not really the Christian view of man but its inaccurate interpretation and inappropriate application! Too often the negative nature of man has been emphasized to the neglect of the positive potential achieved in him through the redemptive activity of God. The law is not balanced by the gospel. Judgment and punishment are experienced more convincingly than divine grace and forgiveness.

Much more could be said about this positive side to round out a more balanced view of man. The human potential actualized through justification by faith, the regeneration of man by the power of the Holy Spirit, the incarnational involvements of God—these are our resources for peace. Indeed, they are more than resources; they are peace!

4.   Economics and Peace

Otto Bremer

The economic causes of war and the economic resources for peace are two sides of one coin. Economic activities and existing economic conditions do, *of course,* have a strong influence on whether war or peace is going to prevail in our world. To change some specific economic reality is to enhance either the chances for peace or the possibility of war, depending on the change that is made. For example, the basic economic reality which influences the possibility of war or peace is that some 20 percent of the world's population has some 80 percent of the world's wealth. Many past wars can be traced to a nation's desire to increase or defend its share of the world's wealth. On the other hand, there is a great resource for peace in efforts to obtain a more just distribution of the world's wealth and resources.

Perhaps the "of course" in the above paragraph is not so obvious to everyone. Few are aware of how much the world of business and economics is indeed a cause of war and a resource for peace. For most people the questions of war and peace are almost instinctively thought of as political issues. Political candidates and office holders are forced to take stands for or against acts of war or programs promising peace. Most advocacy groups for peace address their demands to the political, not the economic powers.

Statements by the churches on war and peace have similarly referred to the political framework; they call for action by legislative bodies and political office holders. Statements by the three largest Lutheran churches in the United States may be typical in this respect: they are almost completely silent with regard to economic factors! As one who has a strong personal and professional interest in the questions of business ethics and economic values, I was surprised to find how easily the economic can be ignored: A statement adopted by my own church a few years ago on Vietnam ignored almost entirely the business/economic dimension of the issue. Except for a reference to the possibility of military funds being better used to alleviate poverty and correct social injustices, there was no position whatever on the substantive economic causes of the conflict or on possible economic actions which might hasten the end of the war.

The lack of interface between business and economics on the one hand and the ethical and moral issues involved in war and peace on the other is one facet of what seems to be a general reluctance on the part of Christians in business and economics to dialogue with theologians and clergy about ethics and values. A few years ago a successful series of "Faith and Life Institutes" brought together persons from the same vocation for ethical reflection. Doctors, lawyers, farmers, politicians, and teachers met in separate convocations with theologians and church leaders to ask questions and seek common answers. Four of the Institutes, however, had to be canceled for lack of participants: one for salesmen, one for corporate executives, one for small businessmen, and one for realtors. Before we attempt to focus attention on the economic dimensions of war and peace it is probably important that we ask why this lack of interface between religion/ethics and business/economics.

The Church and the World of Economics

The late Professor Albert Rasmussen of the Pacific School of Religion once stated with clear insight: "In the tragic separation between religion and life, nowhere is the gap wider than that between faith and the world of economics."[1] He reflected what R. H. Tawney wrote, in his classic *Religion and the Rise of Capitalism,* that "the springs of economic conduct lie in regions rarely penetrated by moralists." Perhaps it is possible, however, even at this late date, to encourage at least some "penetration" —by those who would follow the moral imperatives of the Christian message—into the nature of economic conduct which is either a cause of war or a resource for peace.

If one seeks an historical perspective on the relationship between the church and economic life it is quite clear that at one time religion—specifically Christianity of the twelfth to seventeenth centuries—dominated the whole of life, including the sphere of economics. When "business" was just getting its start, under the aegis of tradesmen and artisans, it was naturally considered subordinate to the more important purpose of the "good life," and was therefore brought under the rule of Christian morality. Readers of Shakespeare will recall the role of the church in dictating what was morally right in commerce. During the Reformation Martin Luther objected to the pope's sanctioning of interest rates and then later made his own pronouncements on what he considered an ethically ac-

1. Albert T. Rasmussen, *Christian Responsibility in Economic Life* (Philadelphia: Westminster, 1965).

ceptable rate. Economics and business have known long periods in which the hand of the church lay heavy upon them.

I recall a conversation of some years ago with Dr. Clark Kerr concerning a suggestion that the church take a greater interest in questions of business ethics and values. The then chancellor of the Berkeley campus of the University of California shook his head and declared, "the last thing we need is some 'Lords Spiritual' trying to dictate business and economic behavior." Much has changed, of course, since the Christian "Lords Spiritual" could dominate the world of economics, but mere possibility of that ever happening again still evokes vigorous reaction in our midst.

There is a kind of cultural memory of the time when religion dominated all of society. One result of this cultural memory has been a determination in the structuring of American life that no one institution should ever dominate all social values. Both Constitution and folk lore have decreed a separation of powers and institutions. The expression "business is business" and the widespread insistence that the churches should concern themselves only with "spiritual" matters represent a popular approval and articulation of the separation. Americans mean to assure a continuing balance—no dominance of one sphere over another.

It is important to recall, however, that the assumptions of classical capitalistic economics were formulated with strong Christian input. At the time he wrote his classic *Wealth of Nations* in 1776 Adam Smith was a professor of moral theology with a specialty in economics! He formulated the four basic assumptions of classical economics:

1) Natural law: as there are laws in physics, such as gravity, so there are God-ordained rules in social relations.

2) Economic man: it is natural for each person to pursue his own economic advantage.

3) Universal competition: it is also a natural law for men to compete with each other.

4) Harmony of interest: fortunately, if each person pursues his or her own interest—if buyers buy as cheap as possible, while sellers sell as high as possible, and if employers pay as low wages as possible while employees seek as high wages as they can get—the result is the best possible society for everyone.

Noteworthy is how greatly these assumptions of classical economics differ from the "good life" presupposed by earlier Christian theology, and how deeply imbedded they are in the thinking of Americans in business and economics.

A student leader of a Vietnam protest in the sixties was asked how he came to hold his radical views; where did he learn them? His answer was immediate: in Sunday school! He went on to say that he first learned the rightness of peace, justice, love, sharing, and forgiveness in his early years of religious training. In later years, however, these ideals took a back seat as the church taught him instead about the sinful, self-centered, competitive, and selfish nature of man.

It is always interesting—and disturbing—to listen to an economist explain business behavior in terms of economic theory: business men seek to maximize their own profit not just for personal advantage but in order that the system can "work" and the "harmony of interests" prevail. In a conspiracy case of the 1950s some major producers of electrical equipment were convicted of price fixing; one of the company executives, as he went to prison, said that what he did may have been illegal but it was surely not unethical. If theologians and ethicists are ever to dialogue with economists and business men on how their activities influence developments toward war and peace, they must first discover some way to break through the traditional assumptions of the "business is business" philosophy.

Historically, the changes in commerce and industry leading to what we now call free enterprise capitalism coincided with the Reformation period. Christians of the Reformation tradition particularly, if they would "seek peace and pursue it," need to have some awareness of the influence of their own tradition on the world of economics. There are at least two classics which trace the relationship: R. H. Tawney's *Religion and the Rise of Capitalism,* which we have already mentioned, and Max Weber's *The Protestant Ethic and the Spirit of Capitalism.* The Calvinist affirmation of capitalism has been particularly influential in America. Financial successes resulting from the economic virtues of achievement, thrift, and hard work were regarded as a sure and tangible sign of one's election and of God's blessing. *Fortune* magazine in its 1950 "Mid-Century" edition used an illustration to indicate how important this Calvinist emphasis has been in American business: If you were an American factory owner under Calvinist influence you would strive to build a bigger factory in order to have on hand a concrete and visible sign of God's enhanced blessing, whereas if you were a factory owner in Germany influenced by Luther you would accept your position as a "calling" given to you by God and seek to live out this vocation responsibly.

The dominance of this particular adaptation of Calvinist

thought has clearly affected the interface of church and economics. It has tended to keep to a minimum any ethical critique of the way in which wealth is obtained, since wealth is regarded as a reward from God. Andrew Carnegie could write in his *Gospel of Wealth* that since God had given him such riches, he had an obligation to be charitable in the way he used it, but not a question was raised about the social and economic justice of the methods by which it was gained. Church statements still fall into the same trap: We appeal to America for sharing its economic wealth with the less fortunate, but we don't inquire at all about the justice of America's having such abundance in the first place. In considering some of the specific points at which economic realities may be a cause of war or a resource for peace, we will seek to avoid the trap.

ECONOMIC ISSUES RELATING TO WAR AND PEACE

The economic conditions and activities which can be a cause of war or a resource for peace, are many in number, and they overlap. Almost every international issue has its economic dimension. Despite the overwhelming complexity of the task, it is important, nonetheless, to delineate some major areas needing attention.

Distribution of Wealth

As long as the "haves" (the 20 percent) of this world become richer and richer at the expense of the poorer "have nots" (the 80 percent), the only alternatives are either continued exploitation by the wealthy nations (backed by the military) or conflict (war) between the "haves" and the "have nots." Despite these ominous alternatives we continue to hear speeches—usually from businessmen—proclaiming that the proof of America's greatness and of the success of American free enterprise is that with only 6 percent of the world's population we have about half of the world's wealth.

Here is a fundamental question which must be faced by anyone concerned about the economic dimension of war and peace: Is the large discrepancy between the disproportionate wealth of the Christian West and the abject poverty of the rest of the world good or bad, desirable or undesirable, just or unjust, conducive to peace or conducive to war? Most Western economists will argue that the need for capital accumulation justifies some people and some nations in being economically better off than the rest. This assumption may now be increasingly open to question as we become aware that world resources are not unlimited.

The *New York Times* of 15 March 1974 gave the following figures from Dr. John Knowles, President of the Rockefeller Foundation: Of the 2.5 billion people who live in the world, 60 percent are malnourished and 20 percent starving. Can we grasp such staggering numbers—500,000,000 persons starving!

Dr. John Bennett has observed that the economic injustice of such lopsided distribution of wealth and resources is the chief mark of brokenness in our world today. He also points to the irony that the majority of the population in the wealthier countries are Christians, at least nominal followers of Jesus Christ. Obviously, the massiveness of the problem calls for global economic strategy. Christians in America—particularly the Christian with expertise in business and economics—must not be satisfied with occasional well-intended, emotionally-based acts of charity. The Christian commitment must rather be to the hard work of developing and implementing a just economic strategy in the global context.

Control of Resources

Increasingly the maldistribution of wealth is seen as a result of the unequal ownership or control of natural resources. The interaction of environmentalists and morally concerned economists and theologians have even given us a new term: eco-justice. As long as it was possible to assume continued rapid growth in the combined gross national products of the countries of the world, it was less imperative to raise questions about the unequal distribution; if the whole pie is getting bigger, each slice it was assumed would be getting bigger also. Most industrialized nations today depend on the Keynesian theory of continued economic growth, with its assumption that gains in one sector trickle down into all the others. Much of the evidence, however, indicates that the results are in fact quite different: while the poor within a given country and the poorer nations throughout the world may have gained somewhat during periods of economic growth, the *gap between* rich and poor has widened exponentially, creating an immense potential for mistrust, social dissolution, and war.

The twofold realization that the world's resources are indeed finite and that the way we have used these resources has done irreparable damage to our very fragile and extremely interdependent eco-system challenges many time-honored assumptions. "Spaceship Earth" symbolizes the awareness that we are mutually dependent upon each other and upon how each uses the limited resources available on our shrinking planet. It is a challenging concept consistent with the vision of world brotherhood.

Garrett Hardin, however, a professor of Human Ecology at the University of California at Santa Barbara, calls the metaphor "suicidal" and suggests that the analogy of lifeboats would be more realistic.[2] Metaphorically, each rich nation amounts to a lifeboat full of comparatively rich people surrounded by masses of struggling poor people in the water nearby, battling and pleading for a chance to survive. To allow the drowning poor into the lifeboat, he suggests, might be complete justice but it would also mean complete catastrophe. The moral position one takes in choosing between the spaceship and the lifeboat images has consequences far beyond the economics of war and peace but certainly crucial in this area as well.

As the poorer nations of the world begin to understand their crisis, their exclusion from the lifeboats in the face of shrinking world resources, it is quite possible, as again Dr. Bennett has noted, that they will see their situation as extremely desperate. Robert Heilbroner envisions the possibility of "wars of pre-emptive seizure" as the imperatives of self-preservation become stronger.[3] The action taken by a desperate nation struggling for survival would be political-military in nature, but it would have deep economic roots and its prevention would necessitate economic solutions. Some economic actions are matters of national political decision, of course, but many more are the result of individual corporate decisions and these need to be looked at.

2. Garrett Hardin, *Population, Evolution, and Birth Control,* 2nd ed. (San Francisco: W. H. Freeman and Co., 1969), pp. 87 ff., and see especially "Lifeboat Ethics: The Case Against Helping the Poor," *Psychology Today* (September 1974), p. 39.
3. Robert L. Heilbroner, *Between Capitalism and Socialism* (New York: Random House, 1970), pp. 282 ff.

Overseas Investment and Multinational Corporations

Many have optimistically predicted that increased worldwide commercial interaction and the emerging multinational corporations will so internationalize the world that wars will be ruled out. There is certainly support for such optimism. It seems quite clear that the economic considerations of American corporations—including agribusiness—were very important in the establishment of detente between the United States and China and Russia. The *New Yorker* magazine recently quipped that the rich Arab countries were investing so much in the United States that it would soon be in their economic self-interest to keep the oil flowing to America.

Before the conclusion is firmly drawn that increased international trade is totally a resource for peace, it is well to remember that commercial relationships between developed and developing nations have always been to the advantage of the developed country. When the richer nations needed raw materials, these were extracted from the poor nations. When industrial changes and new synthetics reduced the need for raw materials, the developing countries were abandoned—until higher labor costs and unionization at home sent the corporations back seeking cheap labor. Decisions were almost universally made in terms of the advantage to the developed country. Lothar Hock of Brazil said during a recent visit to the United States: "The normal American still thinks of his country as being the savior of the world. He does not realize that we in Brazil—our cheap labor and natural resources— are being used to raise the standard of living in this country."[4]

4. Lothar Hock, News Bureau of National Lutheran Council USA, 2 November 1973.

While it is true that multinational corporations have drawn the business communities of countries closer together, this has often been at the expense and to the detriment of the poorer people. As the *Wall Street Journal* reported concerning Indonesia: "Money pours in, yet it doesn't seem to trickle to the great masses of people."[5] In economic terms, it may be that the rich in the United States and the rich in overseas countries do get richer but the poor do not benefit. The realization of this fact may well have inflamed the internal class struggle which contributed to the Vietnam war.

The presence in foreign countries of increased numbers of American corporation people at the same time that the number of Americans associated with embassies, information centers, libraries, and the Peace Corps is declining may even be changing significantly our sources of information and the nature of our communications channels. For example, while there are 737 American executives in the United Kingdom presiding over corporations controlling 10 percent of the net worth of all United Kingdom corporations, there are only 122 officers in the American Embassy in London. It is clearly possible that "American Interest" abroad will be influenced heavily by data supplied by people concerned chiefly with business and economic considerations.

It is a potential resource for peace that so many of the stockholders in American corporations doing business overseas are members of Christian churches in the United States. A task force studying mission on six continents concluded that if the American people knew the detrimental effects of overseas investments, they would object. Perhaps they would, but not likely. Even responsible

5. *Wall Street Journal,* 26 February 1974, p. 1.

church authorities investing, for example, church pension funds seem unable to use any criteria other than maximum dollar return. With United States investments in South Africa returning 18.2 percent in 1969 (compared to 12.2 percent worldwide) the "prudent man" principle of trusteeship will dictate the continuance of such investments whether or not they contribute to economic injustice and the potential for conflict. With perhaps 40 to 50 percent of corporate stock now held by institutional investors (banks, mutual funds, pension funds, foundations) and with the increased evidence that investment officers are unwilling to give even small consideration to the social consequences of corporate action either at home or overseas, it seems likely that corporate managers will feel free to concentrate on maximizing profit and ignore criticisms of policies and actions which are potentially a cause of war. To the credit of many denominations, however, the hope of influencing peace and justice by raising questions concerning social justice with stockholders and corporate officials has not been abandoned.

Finally, it may be observed how little check there is on how American corporations operate overseas in a small, developing country! At home corporate behavior is circumscribed by law, labor unions, public opinion, and the personal standards of the executives. Overseas it is easy for a corporation to act without the sense of social responsibility which it is increasingly showing at home. The solution probably lies in a combination of increased awareness and commitment by corporate executives to see their executive decisions as a way to "seek peace and pursue it" and increased willingness to allow multinational corporate actions to come under the specific control of international law.

The "Military-Industrial Complex"

Ever since President Eisenhower coined the phrase, there has been much speculation on just how real the "military-industrial complex" is. Obviously there is need for military contractors to have close relationships with the military establishment. Seymour Melman of Columbia University suggests that the military-industrial firm is not autonomous but is controlled by a "state management," by which he means that set of organizations in the Department of Defense which centralizes the management of military industry. The issue may well be more political than economic.

There is evidence that military spending is often used to stabilize the economy. Since it is not responsive to contraction in the private sector, the military budget provides a sort of buffer or balance wheel in the economy. The desirability of such a "balance wheel" can be affirmed, however, without resorting to military production as the device for achieving it. Housing and mass transit in the public sector, for example, could be tackled with the same economic effect.

The question can be raised about the extent to which firms engaged in military production still operate as normal business firms, for example, struggling to sell their products and to increase sales and revenue. To succeed, any firm needs good salesmen. It is instructive in this connection to note that as early as 1959 there were 768 former flag and military officers on the payrolls of 97 of the top 100 defense contractors. If a military-industrial firm can convince the military that a certain number of trident ballistic missile submarines—at 1.3 billion each— are necessary for a proper national defense posture, a good sale has been made. If the existence of peace or an improvement in international relations results in nonuse of certain products, it also unleashes economic pressures to create an artificial demand—even war. David Bagelon has observed that "war, and only war, solves the problem of inventory."

The issue here is not whether as a nation we should have an adequate defense capacity—I believe that we must. The issue rather is whether economic considerations should be allowed to function as a potential cause of war, whether the needs of the economy should rank so high that war itself is considered "justified" if it contributes to economic stability and health.

Perhaps the basic question has to do with the purpose and meaning of human existence. If the meaning of life consists in the competitive struggle—where I know that if you lose, I win—then the issue is simply whether war is a desirable means to make sure that I win. If, however, we are able to accept a vision of brotherhood and cooperation—and are willing to start where we are and to work hard and without letup—than it is possible to make economic cooperation a valid resource for peace. If economic energy and know-how can be enlisted to solve the tremendous social and human problems we face at home and abroad, there will no longer be the pressure to look to military contracts and even to war as the key to economic survival.

The Sanctity of Private Property

In discussing the issues raised above we posed no question about the continuation of free enterprise capitalism as known in America; much can be done within the established socio-economic framework. But Christian freedom should enable us to ask basic questions even about

private property and about the extent to which its existence or abolishment may be a cause of war or a resource
for peace.

Serious concern over the economic dimension of war
and peace can leave no question unprobed, no aspect
untouched. Clearly, the day to day activities of American
business have consequences far beyond the narrow world
of economics. And for Christians in America, particularly
those who exercise power in corporate/economic decision-
making, it is no longer enough to respond to the economic
needs of the world with emotionally motivated acts of
charity. There must be a long-range and hard-nosed commitment to the excruciatingly difficult task of devising and
implementing a just economic strategy as a resource for
peace in the global context.

5.   Politics and Peace

Ralph L. Moellering

Public opinion polls repeatedly demonstrate that many Americans are extremely pessimistic about the possibilities for achieving and preserving peace in the foreseeable future. Inured to a prolonged cold war with the USSR, and disillusioned by the Vietnam debacle, they seem to anticipate perpetual international discord and major or minor outbursts of violence in various parts of the globe.

THE DIVERSITY OF FACTORS RELATING TO WAR

Economic realities, psychological conditioning, and theological misconceptions all combine with political factors to make peace appear illusory and wars inevitable. The national budget now envisions using about 60 percent of the income tax dollar to pay for wars—past, present, and future. The United States has spent about $1.5 trillion on the military since World War II. Weapons are supplied to regimes in South America and elsewhere which promise to protect our corporate interests and the overseas investments of wealthy citizens. Moreover, any action to curb military expenditures seems likely to have adverse economic repercussions. Even congressmen opposed to inflated arms budgets are likely to favor the retention of local defense production plants which provide jobs for their constituents.

Psychologically, we all tend to assume that conflict is

natural and nonviolence abnormal. Parents buy their children all sorts of miniature models of death-dealing devices. Supposedly innocuous toy guns and tanks actually influence youngsters to accept at an early age war games which they can act out with utter seriousness in later life, when they volunteer or are drafted into the armed forces. The imaginary battles of childhood are all too readily transformed into the gruesome slaughter of fellow human beings labeled as "enemies." Education for peace is minimal or nonexistent in our schools. Recruiters for the Marines can stress the opportunities provided by the corps to display physical prowess and brute strength. Recruiters for the Navy can delude restless youth, eager to prove their masculinity, with the prospect of exotic and daring adventures in faraway places. Every big league baseball game is preceded by the intoning of an anthem about "bombs bursting in air."

Politicians are also products of the preconditioning which they receive in typical American schools and homes, in which patriotism includes assent to war-making. An entire generation of candidates for political office, since 1945, has regarded it as advantageous to claim honorable service to the country during World War II.

Generally speaking, the churches have been reliable allies in endorsing governmental military ventures. Politicians and clergymen have often concurred in the resort to forceful intervention to settle disputes. Faulty biblical interpretations in particular have aided statesmen by undergirding their bellicose inclinations. For a nation at war, there have been abundant "proof texts" from the Sacred Writings to provide a moral rationale for inflicting casualties. "Holy war" as defined in the book of Deuteronomy and waged by the ancient Israelites has usually been applied by churchmen to the conflicts in which "Christian" America has upheld the cause of divine righteousness. Pacifism has often been dismissed as utopian sentimentalism which contradicts the admonition of Jesus: "Take heed that no one leads you astray. . . .'You will hear of wars and rumors of wars. . . . For nation will rise against nation, and kingdom against kingdom . . ." (Matt. 24:4-7). With an almost fatalistic acceptance of the normality of incessant war, much religious piety assumes that it is futile—even anti-Scriptural—to become concerned about eradicating the causes of conflict. Thus, some types of theologizing blend with prevalent economic and psychological factors to become serious obstacles to the search for peace. The prophetic portrayal of a future era in which swords would be beaten into plowshares and spears into pruning hooks, and in which the fear of violence would be banished is dismissed as allegorical hyperbole, irrelevant to *Realpolitik.* Somehow, the beatitude which extols the peacemakers as potential sons of God is never taken seriously as a mandate for actual involvement in political strategies which might lessen the risk of war and enhance the opportunities for nonviolent alternatives.

Theology can, however, be applied in an altogether different way, so that Christians are encouraged to enter the political arena and to struggle—with a measure of hope and optimism—to accelerate nuclear disarmament and the renunciation of war. In endeavoring to propound *A Theology of Politics,* William Lazareth begins by perceiving that "God wills both peace and justice for our political life together." Our foremost objectives, he avers, must be to find ways and means of resisting "ruthless tyranny" while simultaneously "avoiding the horrors of total nuclear war." To achieve these ends, it is indispensable that the Christian exert a beneficial influence within the political sphere, even though he dare never become oblivious to his dual citizenship, which includes membership in the kingdom of God. Never does he anticipate perfect solutions, or the "Christianizing" of politics. Constantly aware of the paradoxical tension involved in belonging to both church and state, he uses faith to illumine reason and love to enlighten justice. Congruently, the Christian is "always careful to distinguish the religious 'peace of God' from the political peace among the nations." In faithful witness to the kingdom of God, he is obligated to struggle against "the corporate lust for power we call war." Responding to the Prince of Peace who established spiritual and eternal peace with God for the benefit of all of humanity, he possesses a profound motivation for energetically proceeding with his peace-making vocation.[1]

THE POLITICS OF WAR

As he undertakes his God-given task, the discerning Christian will soon detect that one of the political factors which contributes to war-making is to be found on the domestic front. It is the problem which office-holders have if they want to succeed in being reelected. Even when individual congressmen clearly recognize that certain military actions are unnecessary or undesirable, they may feel compelled to conform with majority opinion or even succumb to an emotional outburst of pseudopatriotic fervor because they are unwilling to jeopardize their own future careers in government. Not to support a call-to-

1. See William H. Lazareth, *A Theology of Politics* (Philadelphia: LCA Board of Social Ministry, 1965).

arms in a time of crisis leaves the dissenter open to an accusation of disloyalty. If the congressman belongs to the same political party as the incumbent president, negative votes on foreign policy measures proposed by the administration may be interpreted as serious breaches of party discipline, detracting from the needed display of party unity. On the other hand, if a congressman belongs to the opposition party during a war and speaks or acts contrary to the chief executive, he is likely to be charged with a narrow sense of partisanship and a foolhardy unwillingness to overlook party affiliations when a united stand is crucial for national security.

Most disturbing is the tendency of most members of the Congress to continue to support a war, once it has been declared or is in progress, no matter how much evidence accumulates to demonstrate that it is wrong or contrary to the best interests of the nation. For the citizenry to become incensed over the belligerent policies of a president once a war has been instigated is extremely unlikely, both because it violates the tradition of standing by the head of state when embroiled with a foreign antagonist, and because the incumbent president has enough propaganda devices at his disposal to influence public opinion in his favor. Quite understandably, then, there is not enough pressure from the grass roots to compel Congress to countermand the decisions of the chief executive. Exercising its power of the purse, the legislative branch of the government could nullify an ill-considered act of militancy, or rigidly delimit the scope of any military operation. However, as long as the majority of the population accepts the apologetics for war-making offered by a president— or simply remains silent—the Congress cannot be expected to take a courageous stand by voting to withhold funds.

Two striking examples may be found in the Mexican War and in the Vietnam War. Reputable historians today appear to be unanimous in condemning our abuse of our neighbor south of the Rio Grande in the 1840s. Careful research has verified the allegation that our expansionist impulse caused us to take ruthless advantage of a neighboring country's weaknesses for the purpose of territorial aggrandizement. Our own provocative actions goaded the Mexicans into a skirmish in which a few of our soldiers were killed. Immediately, the outcry was that American blood had been shed on American soil. A bill was drawn up which would authorize the president to accept militia and volunteers for military duty. To give formal recognition to a state of war, a preamble was added which read: "Whereas, by the act of . . . Mexico, a state of war exists between that government and the United States . . . [the president is empowered to use whatever means are necessary to bring the war to a successful conclusion]."

That preamble was greeted with instant denunciation. The Whig press declared that it was defiling falsehood which assumed that the war was defensive when patently it was aggressive—forced on Mexico by President Polk. Charles Francis Adams, grandson of the second president of the United States, pronounced the preamble "one of the grossest national lies that was ever deliberately told." Nevertheless, stampede tactics pushed the war bill through the House, two hours after it was received, by a vote of 174 to 14. In the Senate, the lopsided vote was 40 to 2.

Once the war was approved, positions regarding its legitimacy and morality were determined largely by political affiliation. The Whigs, north and south, were extremely critical of the war. The administration Democrats supported it. Conservatives among the northern Whigs emphasized the fraud and the aggressiveness of the war; the radicals added the charge that the primary aim of the administration was the extension of slavery. Conspicuous expansionists and war hawks among the Democrats believed that it was the "manifest destiny" of the United States to expand over the entire continent of North America; therefore, the absorption of Mexican territory could be justified. The Democrats, however, embraced a large minority of antislavery radicals and a number of old-fashioned Jeffersonians who might have been expected to object to the war.

In view of the diversity in both parties, and the considerable direct opposition to an attack on Mexico, how can one explain the overwhelming vote by which Congress endorsed the war? The explanation can be found in the momentary hysteria on the part of the public which Polk intentionally converted into a steamroller to stifle any possible resistance to his objective. It was a normal popular response to what was understood as an assault on the flag. Party loyalties and the appeal to national solidarity during wartime prevented both Democrats and Whigs from resisting the prevailing policy. The Whigs did not function because they feared the political consequences. If they voted against the war declaration, they would meet the fate which had overtaken their predecessors, the Federalists, who were obliterated from the political scene by their opposition to the War of 1812. Even though many Whigs denounced the war as iniquitous and unconstitutional, they regularly voted supplies and men for the fighting.[2] Dubious Democrats were quiescent because their

2. Even John Quincy Adams, who labeled the war unconstitutional, did not want to be accused of withholding material from the armies. Abraham Lincoln, who entered Congress in 1847 and

leaders had sponsored the joint resolution annexing Texas —a resolution which had helped provoke the war.

The deplorable reality is that any congressman hesitating to vote in favor of financing a war is likely to be accused of subverting his country's security. A war, right or wrong, once it has been entered into by a vote of Congress must be upheld. Soldiers at the front must not be endangered by any moral scruples on the part of the lawmakers which would induce them to withhold funds for weapons and ammunition.[3]

Disturbing parallels to the Mexican War can be found over a hundred years later in the Vietnam disaster. Real motives were camouflaged beneath pious pretensions and misleading propaganda. At various times, our intervention was disguised as a humanitarian venture, an effort to establish a model democracy in Southeast Asia, or as an essential defense against communist aggression.

Initially, we aided the French in their attempt to restore their colonial rule over Indochina. After their defeat and withdrawal, we contributed to the ascendancy of the tyrant Diem and enabled him to block fulfillment of that provision in the Geneva Accords of 1954 which called for nationwide "free" elections. When it became apparent that Ho Chi Minh might succeed in unifying all of Vietnam, we contrived the Gulf of Tonkin incident to find an excuse for a punitive action against him. In an emotional

registered his protest against the war, regularly voted supplies for it.
3. Frederick Merk of Harvard University delineated this problem in his writing on "Dissent in the Mexican War." Together with essays on the War of 1812 and the Spanish-American War by his colleagues Samuel Eliot Morison and Frank Freidel, it was published under the title *Dissent in Three American Wars* (Cambridge: Harvard University Press, 1970).

mood not dissimilar to that which preceded the Mexican War, Congress hurriedly and almost unanimously passed the notorious Gulf of Tonkin resolution. When it was reported that American warships had been fired upon, it was assumed that retaliation should be endorsed. Thereafter, Presidents Johnson and Nixon claimed that every step of escalation in the war by executive decree was only a logical and legal implementation of the original congressional action. Even without an official declaration of war, it was imagined that the Commander-in-Chief of the Armed Forces had a right to issue whatever orders were necessary to safeguard American interests.

With these questionable presuppositions, we proceeded to engage in the brutal counterinsurgency search-and-destroy tactics which devastated the Vietnamese countryside and exterminated countless noncombatants. Air raids wiped out entire villages. Casualties included women and children. The cumulative total tonnage dropped on Indochina eventually amounted to more than three times that dropped in all theaters of operation in World War II. Defying the U.N. Charter and incurring denunciations from countries all over the world, we stubbornly persisted in our unilateral intervention until it became obvious that we were doomed to failure.[4]

As never before, a large percentage of Americans became disillusioned about a war venture, and criticism spread to Congress. However, senators and representatives could not deny that they had voted in favor of the Gulf of Tonkin resolution, and they felt obligated, time after time, to underwrite military expenditures. As in the Mexi-

---

4. For documentary evidence and opinions on the war in Southeast Asia, cf. Marvin E. Gelleman, ed., *Vietnam* (Greenwich, Conn.: Fawcett, 1965).

can War, it was unthinkable to withhold adequate equipment and supplies from our fighting men. No matter how convinced a congressman became that the Vietnam War was a ghastly mistake, he seemed powerless to stop it because he could not risk his political career by daring to vote against military appropriations. Even the most vociferous doves usually fell in line.

It is precisely in the face of this situation that thoughtful Christians can and must assume a serious and significant responsibility. Instruction for peace in the churches should include familiarizing people with those provisions of the Constitution that curb the war-making prerogatives of the president. Perhaps constitutional amendments or clearcut legislation should be introduced to make it impossible or unlikely in the future that a crisis situation can propel us into another unjust or futile war because our legislators are blinded by false propaganda, or pressured by a frenzied public reaction to unverified and exaggerated reports of external hostility.

Perspectives on Foreign Policy

If we are to change direction and begin to examine the possibilities for a stable and just peace throughout the world, it becomes of paramount importance for us to scrutinize recent perspectives on foreign policy in relation to American politics. Lowell Livezey, Executive Director of the World Without War Council-Midwest, has distinguished four positions which have been advocated in the last few decades. Two of them, he claims, have been operative in every administration since World War II: liberal internationalism and power realism.

Beginning with Woodrow Wilson's vision of a world of civilized men, lip service at least has been paid to the ideal of restraining conflict and adjudicating international rivalries. In terms of specific policy, liberal international-ism, according to Livezey, is committed to:

> . . . strengthening the United Nations and using it for the resolution of disputes, assisting in rapid economic develop-ment and enhancing economic justice, recognizing basic human rights and safeguarding them through international law, courts and enforcement mechanisms, reaching agree-ment with adversaries on arms control and eventual gen-eral disarmament with international inspection and con-trol, building a sense of world community as well as the concrete process for global cooperation in solving common problems.[5]

Power realism, the second approach to foreign policy, is reminiscent of nineteenth-century European diplomacy, which often attempted to cling to a precarious peace by pitting one combination of nations with common interests against another. Shifting alliances and intricate maneuvers resulted in some standoffs between opponents in menacing situations. Before World War I, the British and French governments evolved a close understanding that seemed mutually advantageous. Entering into what was known as an *entente cordiale* with Czarist Russia, they matched the Central Powers—Germany, Austria-Hungary, and Turkey. However, more than ingenious power plays, threats, and counterthreats were needed to prevent a holocaust in 1914. Successive crises could not be averted, and even-tually the alliance system led to irreversible mobilization and an appalling bloodletting.

American diplomacy is acutely aware of the balance of power concept in its delicate and persistent negotiations

5. *Journal of Current Social Issues,* Autumn 1973.

around the globe. With the Warsaw Pact socialist bloc in constant confrontation with the North Atlantic Treaty Organization, both sides are bogged down in overextended military commitments in Europe.[6]

Even worse, the balance of nuclear terror, which continues to be the most ominous peril hovering over all mankind, requires huge expenditures for the maintenance of existing arsenals, and for experimentation with ever more lethal weapons. The Strategic Arms Limitation Treaty agreements notwithstanding, the arms race is not really halted, and a cataclysmic Armageddon is postponed or staved off by the threat of total annihilation. The State Department is apparently committed to constructing a labyrinthine matrix of mutual deterrence among the nations, a Herculean task.

Power realism dictates that detente be maintained between the colossi of the East and the West. It tends to ignore the aspirations of less developed countries which have little power—unless of course they control vast wealth in strategic resources. Power politics may be unavoidable, but if they become cynically Machiavellian, they can have catastrophic consequences in the long run. Faith in the balance of power is inclined to downgrade the importance of international legal and political institutions which might offer viable alternatives to a sheer dependence on nuclear deterrence. Christians need not be naive, starry-eyed idealists. But neither should they surrender Jacob's blessing (God-inspired motifs that could

6. A study prepared by the Friends Committee on National Legislation irreverently asks: "Why are there 75 U.S. generals and admirals serving in the German Federal Republic?" No one expects the Soviets to invade. Yet we spend $3 billion a year to maintain our troops there.

lead to more equity and righteousness) for Esau's pottage (man-devised compromises that betray the poor and the weak).

A third position in relation to foreign affairs is referred to as limited antimilitarism, exemplified by such organizations as SANE (National Committee for a Sane Nuclear Policy) and Americans for Democratic Action. Many liberal churchmen would fit into this category. This perspective focuses attention on the desirability of reducing expenditures for national defense and taking steps in the direction of gradual disarmament. The military budget is often the principal target. "Trimming the fat" may be the expression used. The goal is a "leaner, tougher military." Such limited antimilitarism has usually implied a reordering of priorities with larger appropriations earmarked for grappling with domestic grievances. Sometimes the advocates of this position sound like neo-isolationists. At any rate, they seem to minimize the value of international movements. Christians should be sympathetic to these "moderate" critics of the existing order. For attaining short-term objectives, theirs may be the most promising route to follow.

The fourth category defined by Livezey is revolutionary antiimperialism.[7] Those who reflect this position are firmly convinced that American foreign policy is rooted in capitalist economic structures. Much of their devastating critique is directed against large American corporations,[8]

7. An historical interpretation undergirding this position may be found in William Appleman Williams, *The Tragedy of American Diplomacy* (New York: Dell, 1962).
8. See Tom Christoffel, David Finkelhor and Dan Gilbarg, *Up Against the American Myth* (New York: Holt, Rinehart and Winston, 1970).

although bureaucratic collectivism in the Soviet Union may be castigated just as harshly.

Explicitly siding with the "wretched of the earth," revolutionary antiimperialism provides a significant corrective to the three other positions—all of which, to a greater or lesser degree, tend to be oblivious to the plight of the oppressed. With poignant clarity, the antiimperialists have spotlighted the culpability of U.S. and multinational corporations in aggravating the socio-economic inequalities which, in the end, may make a peaceful world unattainable. The exposés of these iconoclasts compel us to rethink or repudiate our attachment to the existing economic system as we recognize how much it benefits the affluent and penalizes the underprivileged. The deprived masses in Asia, Africa, and Latin America are seething with discontent, violence erupts sporadically, and more bloodshed can be anticipated if the ruling classes turn a deaf ear to every plea for a redistribution of wealth—and if the industrialized nations refuse to help the disgruntled nations.

GLOBAL POSSIBILITIES

Thus, as Livezey intimates, we are presently in a quandary about our national purpose in relation to the rest of the world. The shortcomings and miscalculations of liberal internationalism have induced some observers to question the underlying assumptions that we should actively assist in the creation of global institutions capable of preventing war or that we should continue to offer economic aid to impoverished countries.

Christian love, however, knows no national boundaries, and will always seek to alleviate suffering. While perfect justice must await the advent of the kingdom of God in its final fruition, there are remedial measures which can be introduced as a deliberately planned movement toward justice evolves. Conflicting concepts about what constitutes justice can be resolved. Disputes between nations can be settled by political means rather than sheer force.

Specifically, a global system which outlaws war and provides for a lawful appraisal of contested claims is, in principle, just as feasible as the legal devices which restrain and provide alternatives to violence within the nation-states. Undoubtedly such a system would depend upon a complex set of international agreements, but the United States could take the initiative in proposing and backing such agreements.

Writing in *Foreign Affairs* in 1949, Reinhold Niebuhr was too discouraged by "Russian intransigence" to imagine that any plan for world government could be implemented. The desire to move beyond the nation-state to a world community with a functioning constitutional structure seemed too limited.[9] Almost thirty years later, however, we can be more receptive to proposals for overcoming a narrow-minded, obsolete nationalism with "one world" blueprints. A totally disarmed world with adequate international inspection and control is not a chimerical vision.[10]

Small beginnings now could lead to rapid progress later. More imaginative and daring steps could be taken— even unilateral actions—which would reduce or stabilize

9. See Reinhold Niebuhr, "The Illusion of World Government," reprinted in *Christian Realism and Political Problems* (New York: Scribner's, 1953), p. 17: "The fallacy of world government can be stated in two simple propositions. The first is that governments are not created by fiat. . . . The second is that governments have only limited efficacy in integrating a community."

10. See Arthur N. Holcombe, *A Strategy of Peace in a Changing World* (Cambridge: Harvard University Press, 1967).

the level of armaments. Bold efforts could be made to advance multilateral agreements to strengthen the United Nations and all of its agencies. Throughout, the church's vigorous support should be given to "Bread for the World," a nonpartisan political lobby dedicated to such specific objectives as fair trade, "investment without empire," and financing the development of resources in poor countries.[11] Top priority, as an investigating congressional committee recently testified, must be given to rescuing the impoverished masses of the Third World from starvation and disaster. In 1969, U Thant said:

> I do not wish to seem overdramatic, but I can only conclude from the information available to me as Secretary-General that the members of the United Nations have perhaps ten years left in which to subordinate their ancient quarrels and launch a global partnership to curb the arms race, to improve the human environment, to defuse the population explosion, and to supply the required momentum to world development efforts.[12]

The determination expressed in the U.N. Charter in 1945 "to save succeeding generations from the scourge of war" should be reaffirmed. The "impossible" must become possible. What may appear remote and difficult to attain has become urgent necessity.

11. For full information, address Bread for the World, 602 E. Ninth Street, New York, New York 10009.
12. Quoted by Paul and Arthur Simon, *The Politics of World Hunger* (New York: Harper's Magazine Press, 1973), pp. 220-21.

6.   On Not Leaving It to the Pacifists

Charles P. Lutz

Before I suggest some points for the agenda of Christians concerned about peace, I would ask that you look with me at where we're headed as Christians today, particularly in the United States, on issues of world peace. Where are we now? Where ought we be moving? What are the major theological questions before us? And what are the agenda items we need to pick up if we want to get to work?

THE CHANGING CHRISTIAN CONSCIOUSNESS

We usually talk about building toward the future on the basis of a previous experience. Military planners do that. People who work for peace do that too. This means that there has probably been some positive fallout from the American experience in Vietnam— that it has begun to change the consciousness of Christians and perhaps of Americans generally. Let me mention briefly three ways in which that has happened, all positive:

1) Warfare is now an ethical question worthy of attention even by nonpacifist churches. That was not the case twenty years ago. During the Korean period, when I was in college and seminary, we were effectively sheltered from the draft question. In an entire ethics course at the seminary during the mid-fifties we spent one portion of one hour talking about the war/peace question. That was it—that's all I remember hearing on the subject in four

years of seminary education. It was simply not a central question, even though the cold-warring and hot-warring were both going on at the time. During that decade American Christians took for granted the legitimacy of warfare. We no longer do that today, and that's a gift—a beneficial fallout from the Vietnam experience.

2) The just-war ethic is no longer adequate for many of us who once took it for granted—if indeed we ever really knew what it was. Looking back historically, we find that it has seldom been tried, but when it has been tried it has been found wanting. National leaders have generally ignored its criteria; churches have been afraid of pursuing its implications. Thus, the whole ethical framework that Christians used as a rationale for taking part in war is now subject to severe questioning. And that's partly because in the Vietnam conflict the just-war ethic didn't help us very much, except in after-the-fact analysis. It didn't help either in preventing war or in shaping the conduct of it.

3) The tendency among American Christians to idolatrize their government has been seriously undermined, and the biblical Christian can only greet this as a positive development. The former tendency to think of government as incapable of doing wrong, and to regard its claims and mandates as absolute and beyond question, has also been undermined by the Vietnam trauma—and that's a gain. Of course, Watergate has contributed to this more realistic assessment as well, for Watergate and the government's great need to look good are closely related.

The Emerging Ethical Questions

Now, where do we go theologically and ethically? Four points may be mentioned.

Violence

We need to look anew at the whole question of violence. To me, it is disturbing that some of us who are finally ready to throw out the just-war ethic as not very helpful, are at the same time eager to accept a just-revolution ethic. We seem willing in some situations to say that the criteria for a just-war may be applied to justify a revolution which uses violence as a last resort. I do feel uncomfortable with that. The churches are not ready to settle the question yet, but we can't put off grappling with it. Is violence ever legitimate? Under what circumstances? If it's not legitimate in terms of war between nations, is it legitimate in revolutionary settings— within a community of people? There are three broad opinions about that:

1) There's the situation of those already in a violent setting, who have themselves been the recipients of violence, for example, people in southern Africa or Latin America or Northern Ireland. The challenge for Christians there is: how to live with the situation, how to humanize the conflict, how to bring order and build structures of peace in the midst of a violent situation.

2) Violent resistance is sometimes a necessity in extreme circumstances, the criteria for which are somewhat akin to those of the just-war ethic.

3) Nonviolent resistance to unjust political and economic power is the only course consistent with obedience to Jesus Christ.

Now, most Christians have not even begun to talk about those questions yet, much less reached a position concerning them. I don't know that we need to have a single position on the question of violent revolution, but I do know that we need to grapple with it.

Church and State

We need also to look at the question of country versus conscience much more than we have. Martin Marty says that when the crunch comes Americans—and especially Christians—have usually put country ahead of conscience. The Christian witness has traditionally been toward obedience. On church-state questions, obedience to government has historically been our slogan. We have been much less than prophetic over against Caesar's standard-bearers.

We need to be reminded that early Christians refused military service largely because of the state worship implicit in it. Scriptures say that the state has no absolute claim on us—its sovereignty is not complete. In one sense Jesus broke the sovereignty of Rome by going to the cross. By the cross he defeated the principalities and powers. His followers understood themselves as called to pursuing a similar course.

Though we may not like their theology, Jehovah's Witnesses are telling us something important in their absolute rejection of the absolute authority of the state. Visitors to the United States from six continents recently had some significant things to say on the same point. After observing church life here for a month, they told us that the American church, perhaps unconsciously, is more identified with the state than is the church in Europe, where for centuries the relationship between the two had legal standing. And they scored our use of nationalist symbols in our churches—the flag in the chancel—and our uncritical acceptance of the current way of ministering to military personnel through the in-uniform chaplaincy.

Pacifism

We must in addition take a serious look at the pacifist option. Most Christians have never really taken seriously the pacifist witness. We have not really dialogued with the peace-church Christians. John Howard Yoder's book, *The Politics of Jesus,* is one that can broaden understanding of the pacifist option and, in fact, of the whole social message of the New Testament.[1]

There is little argument among social ethicists and theologians that nonresisting love is the ethic of Jesus. Was Jesus a pacifist? Maybe the term "pacifist" is not the most helpful, because we have a narrow understanding of what that means. But Jesus' ethic for himself and for his followers was nonresisting love.

Reinhold Niebuhr felt that this stance was appropriate for individual Christians but that in a world of evil it is not appropriate for governments or for bodies of citizens. Yoder argues that Christians cannot separate their personal and their public ethical behavior. He sees Jesus rejecting four standard ways of relating to society: Jesus clearly rejected the Zealot or revolutionary option. He also rejected the option of the chaplain who functions within the system to perform religious ministrations and never really asks any troublesome questions. He rejected the option of quietism. The quietist moves not in constant paradox with his culture—as Luther said the Christian must—but in a kind of paralysis alongside the culture, coexisting with but in detachment from his culture. Or he exists parallel with his culture, each going its own separate way—which is how Luther's two-kingdoms image is often misinterpreted. Finally, Yoder says, Jesus rejected the option of withdrawal or retreat.

What he did choose, according to Yoder—and this opened up a whole new understanding for me—was a

1. John Howard Yoder, *The Politics of Jesus* (Grand Rapids: Eerdmans, 1972).

wholly new way, the path of suffering servanthood, radically open, vulnerable, full of risks, exposed. His way of the cross brings the promise of a new humanity, enabled and given by God.

> It is *par excellence* with reference to enmity between peoples, the extension of neighbor-love to the enemy, and the renunciation of violence even in the most righteous cause, that this promise takes on flesh in the most original, the most authentic, the most frightening and scandalous, and therefore in the most evangelical way. It is the Good News that my enemy and I are united through no merit or work of our own, in a new humanity that forbids henceforth my ever taking his life in my hands.[2]

Building Peace

Whatever ethical route we choose, the goal is peace-nurturing trust, cultivating a wholeness of relationship between peoples—the building of shalom. The purpose is to enhance community between warring groups, or potentially warring groups, of human beings. That is to say, we need peace more than we need pacifism. We need peace-builders more than we need pacifists. This is what Roland Bainton, himself a pacifist, had in mind years ago when he wrote that world peace would not come through the efforts of pacifists alone—they are not numerous enough. World peace would come, rather, through the enlistment of peace-minded nonpacifists—which is really an appeal for the people from the just-war tradition of Christianity to get involved with the struggle for peace and not leave it to the pacifists. Necessary as the pacifist witness is, the pacifists alone will always be a small minority, says Bain-

2. Ibid., pp. 231-32.

ton, and I suspect he's right. But that does *not* excuse the rest of us from getting involved with the endeavor.

It is as if for a long time now most of us Christians have been saying, "Well, the special calling of the peace churches is to hold up the banner for world peace and they do it well; we don't have to." But that will no longer suffice. Bainton is right: if world peace is really to come, it's going to be through the efforts of nonpacifists in vast number joining with the pacifists.

This means, in personal terms, that we go to some root questions. We need to ask about such basic things as how we teach our children about coercion or negotiation, competition or cooperation, safeguarding national security through superior force or taking risks in order to build trust between parties. We can view conflict as contributing to positive growth, not something to be avoided but something to be resolved without destroying the other.

Our challenge is to become leaven in the churches, witnesses for peace and nonviolence. We can form voluntary associations to promote vigorously an idea not yet shared by the larger community in church or world. We can say loudly and with great clarity that organized mass violence will no longer be tolerated as a legitimate form of conduct between nations or groups within nations. At one time there were small voluntary associations of people who said that about slavery. We can call, not for a world in which murder is eliminated—that would be a foolish expectation—but for a world in which mass murder is no longer *lawful*.

THE AGENDA

Now what specifically is our agenda? The greatest problem today is not that some Christians are acting nonviolently for justice and peace while others are resorting to violence. The greatest problem is simply that most Christians are not acting on these matters at all. Most of us are not involved in any way, either violently or nonviolently. Our task as persons concerned about peace is mainly to reach the center in our own churches, not to remain a fringe movement at the left—where any movement is bound to be a pretty thin fringe. The task is to enlist more people and to work at the heart of our Christian communities. Our purpose is not to alienate by saying, "You don't agree with my approach, or my views on the Vietnam war, or on amnesty, so we can't work together." Instead we need to get the message across at the very core of the churches' life that peace-building is the job of every Christian.

There are churchwide study resources available, and more coming, which will help to say just that. These studies and guides need to be used within our congregations.

The nation's bicentennial is coming and we're already building up for an orgy of celebrations of various kinds. But what would be appropriate to the occasion's observance by the religious communities of the nation? The bicentennial affords us an opportunity to look at the heresy of civil religion, at the role of our country in the world community of nations, and at the transnational essence of the Christian message.

We can find ways of giving visible support to brothers and sisters in Namibia, in southern Africa generally, and wherever situations of injustice and violence persist. We can help our fellow Christians on the scene of the struggle to know that someone stands with them—and thereby learn a good deal for ourselves about the situation of others and about our role in their oppression.

We can take care of the unfinished business left over from the Vietnam War here at home. Healing the wounds suffered by all the victims—those who went and those who didn't—and by their families. We can do something about the veterans and their emotional needs, and especially the half million veterans who came out with "bad papers," less than honorable discharges that could stain them socially and legally for life. We can insist that our churches and our government deal with the still unanswered question of rebuilding Indochina, about which the truce agreement also spoke.

Finally, we can form with others into a network—maybe a nationwide network—of groups of people, that would say clearly: Within this communion of Christians there is a passionate concern for the things which make for peace. Such a movement is even now in process of formation. It is being called the Order of St. Martin—after Martin of Tours, Martin Luther, and Martin Luther King, Jr. It hopes to serve as a rallying point for those who seek a support group and a discipline for lifting up God's shalom at every level, from personal relationships to the matters involved in global justice.

Christians are called to witness to shalom—to wholeness in community, healing, harmony, well-being, and commitment to justice. Faithfulness does not require that we be successful in our every attempt to make peace. It does require that we witness to the biblical vision of shalom as God's plan for the single new humanity he has called into being.

7. The Aggressive Pursuit of Peace

Gerald O. Pedersen

We have done some important things in this book, but perhaps nothing more important than this: We have stated that peace is possible. This is a statement of belief. It represents a decision, and a commitment. Many people believe that peace is not possible. The quest is one each Christian will have to decide by himself. If we believe that peace *is* possible, then we must not only affirm the conviction but commit ourselves to it unreservedly. We must not be turned back for any reason whatever when the call is to "seek peace and pursue it." I invite and challenge you, the reader, to make this commitment.

OBSTACLES TO PEACE

There are many obstacles in the way. We have mentioned only a few of them. First, and perhaps the most important obstacle, is the fact that the achievement of peace is such a difficult, enormous, and complex undertaking. Sheer bewilderment at the scope of the task can itself be enough to discourage us. But we know that whatever is most worthwhile is nearly always most difficult and that its difficulty—its seeming improbability—ought not turn us off. Most of us believe that the kingdom of God cannot be realized by our efforts but must be given by God; yet this should not stop us from full, total, and unconditional commitment toward its realization.

Another obstacle to peace is that the church has to a large extent been part of the problem, rather than part of the solution. Rather than being empowered by the kingdom and directed by the word of God, we have too often been captured by our culture and its dictates. Ignoring Scripture, we have become culturally conservative. That is, we have listened to and sanctioned the culturally popular attitudes regarding war, national purpose, and public ethics, conserving all that has been passed on to us by our society. We should instead have been biblically conservative, listening to and preserving the biblical concept, vision, and experience of shalom.

THE CHURCH AS A RESOURCE FOR PEACE

In this book we have looked at some of the major economic, political, and psychological obstacles to peace. In each of these areas the church could discern great possibilities for peace building. But for this to happen we Christians will have to *be* the *church,* faithful to our best understanding of ourselves as people of God.

Economics

The economic inequalities and inequities that exist among the people of the earth are one of the major threats to a peaceful planet. 80 percent of the wealth is at the disposal of 20 percent of the population. This fact alone threatens constantly to disrupt the tenuous balances established to forestall open conflict; it generates pressures in the direction of rebellion and war. Beyond that, the misery of the masses of hungry, ill-housed, sick, illiterate, and unemployed is a constant witness that peace itself is lacking in their lives—and if in their lives, then in ours, too.

Biblical vision requires us to cry out that the mere

absence of open warfare is *not* peace, for shalom requires full realization of human potential, vigor of life, wholeness, and opportunity—and these the poor of the earth do not have. The church is concerned, not only because the suffering masses demand that something be done, and because their plight is a threat to world peace. The church has at the center of its concern a Christ-like compassion for the poor, the hungry, and the needy. Whether anyone else is sensitive to their cries or not, the church is, and it does have this compassion. "Blessed are those who hunger, for they shall be filled." To ignore one of these "little ones" is to ignore the Lord himself, whose injunction is to "feed my people." The church, by its very nature, is one international agency that is committed to the just and equitable distribution of the world's goods to every person and nation.

The church's vision of world brotherhood moves it to accept seriously the symbol of "spaceship earth," with its reminder of each one's interdependence with all others and of the necessity for sharing responsibly the limited resources available in our single planetary eco-system. Even where the rich nations are seen as "life boats," surrounded by teaming masses of struggling and perishing poor people—who would capsize the boats for all were they allowed to come aboard—the church, manifesting the compassion of its Lord, is obligated to raise moral questions about the whole situation and to search for alternative solutions in which justice is not ignored. Shalom requires this much at least. And the church, bearing the marks of Christ, can settle for nothing less.

Politics

Politically, the obstacles to peace are many. American voters are preoccupied with our own favored position in world affairs, our control over third-world development, our multinational corporations and their profits round the world, the political and economic benefits of military appropriations and even of warmaking.

The whole concept of nationalism, which is growing vigorously as the underdeveloped nations get on with their nation-building, seems totally archaic and short-sighted among the powerful nations. Appropriate perhaps in an earlier period of history, it shrinks the loyalties of planetary citizens on a shrinking globe.

The church could be a fantastic resource for peace in the political sphere because the church is an international and ecumenical body. It recognizes no limits—national, racial, or otherwise—except this: that we are God's people, reflections of Christ, and meant to be a light to the whole world. As God's all-inclusive people, we will bow down to no nation-state, no ideology. Of course, we may need some liberation ourselves before we come to that commitment. The churches we belong to are largely captive to narrow thinking, limited political loyalties, inherited and often unexamined social and cultural values. The only real question before us is this: Will we be the church or not? Will we believe and proclaim that God alone is sovereign, that there is only one Lord of History, and that our ultimate commitment can never be to any lesser authority?

Psychology

Psychologically, we must acknowledge the pessimism operating in many Christian circles, the dehumanizing and immobilizing concepts of all-pervasive sinfulness, the hang-ups we have about authority—especially the governing authorities—as sacrosanct, the baleful influence of our defensive mechanisms in life, and our quietistic attitudes toward social concerns.

But what a tremendous resource our faith could be psychologically were we to speak about transformation, conversion, growth, new creation, freedom, and responsibility, and about the dignity and glory of man—as much as we do about human sinfulness. That human nature is sinful, and violence a common experience, need not make war inevitable. War is primarily a social phenomenon, not a matter of personal ethics. If we have learned to resolve most national or domestic conflicts thru legal and non-violent means, why not international conflicts as well? Besides, shalom is not the mere absence of conflict but the positive fullness and vigor of life, including in its majestic wholeness all life's stresses and tensions. Psychologically, we need not be pessimistic, we can be optimistic, because satan does not control our planet—the earth is the Lord's!

Toward a Peace Ethic

In this book no final peace ethic has been suggested because that will remain a continuing task. But several things have become quite clear. First, even on the basis of the older justifiable war ethic to which most Christians hold, whether knowingly or unknowingly, we must insist that war is wrong. Unless in very exceptional cases where under the most careful scrutiny it meets certain quite specific conditions, participation in violence must be presumed to be wrong. And war, which is legalized violence, must similarly be presumed from the outset to be wrong. We have usually gone at the matter the other way around, presuming that *our* war is right unless somebody can dream up a good reason why we should *not* engage in it.

But in principle, war is always wrong, and the burden of proof is on those who contend that a particular war is not.

We had better remind ourselves too, we who still affirm the justifiable war position, that on the basis of the same criteria justifiable revolt and justifiable revolution are also possible. The outcasts of the earth, those 80 percent of all earthmen who possess 20 percent of the earth's wealth, probably have a more legitimate right than we to regard their violence as justifiable. Recognizing that the poor have a more valid claim than we to be engaged in a "just war," and that in 99 percent of the cases the ethical criteria for the just war are never actually used, much less properly applied, where "our cause" is at stake —it is automatically presumed to be right—we Christians should demand a theological reconsideration of the church's traditional war ethic and the formulation of a modern and workable peace ethic.

In this connection we need to reconsider the pacifist position. Its major emphasis is not a negative rejection of killing as such but a positive commitment to peace-building above all. Long before the question of war arises, it seeks aggressively to promote peace and to restrain evil. Surely that must also be our commitment, to be so aware of injustice in its early stages that we organize to combat it, lest by our default justifiable violence—war—becomes the only option available. We cannot leave it to the pacifist any longer to promote alternatives to war.

A final word to those who, rejecting pacifism and the just-war theory, insist on the holiness of the cause which has marked America's struggles around the world in the last decade (or half century): Is this protracted holy war, whether in its hot or cold stages, this crusade that we have been supporting, really His business? carried on in the name of the righteous God? Or is it perhaps preserved rather in the name of national self-interest? Freedom? Democracy? Power? Mistaken pride? Can we ever use the techniques of violence on behalf of a messiah who rejected them?

CHRISTIANS AND PEACE

We began the book with certain assumptions, among the first being that what we do here is done in the name of the Man of Peace. We said our purpose is to promote the creation of peace on earth as our response to the Prince of Peace, Jesus Christ, through awakening and informing the people of the church and activating them to follow the biblical injunction to "seek peace and pursue it." We also said, but as an affirmation of faith, that peace is possible. This is our commitment, the faith we seek to share. Christians speak not just of a "way to peace," but of that peace which is "the way," the way to a fulfilled life together in the world "God so loved." Peace is not an absence but a presence. This is why we seek to promote it, speak for it, organize for it. Peace is an active, living thing. I am convinced that if tomorrow or next year or ten or twenty years from now, my older boy in the university, my daughter in high school or my younger boy in kindergarten or anybody else's son—or daughter—in this country goes to war, a war in which some of "our" people and some of "theirs"—all alike *God's* people—die, it will not be because evil had its way, or because the devil caused it. Yes, evil still exists, and the evil one is still very active. But if we go to war, it will be because you and I, Christians with good intentions, were so damned lazy and apathetic that we did not speak out, act, preach, organize, and struggle aggressively to "seek peace and pursue it."

Reading books is not enough—though we're glad you're still with us on this one. Believing in peace is not enough. What is required is that our experience and vision of shalom be lived out in a conscious determination and continuing effort to establish peace at every level of existence—in our personal face-to-face relationships, in the congregations to which we belong, in school and at work, and in the affairs of government, local, state, national, and international. Wherever the Prince of Peace goes before us with his love in our whole world we need to awaken, inform, and activate people—and, whatever the obstacles, never be deterred! This is the aggressive pursuit of peace.

Additional Resources

Bainton, Roland. *Christian Attitudes to War and Peace.* Nashville: Abingdon, 1960. The most useful standard reference on the historical development of pacifism, the "just war," and the crusade.

Brown, Robert McAfee. *Religion and Violence.* Philadelphia: The Westminster Press, 1973. A primer for white, middle-class Americans to sensitize them to the hidden violence in our society—the structural violence built into a status quo created and preserved for the advantage of a small minority.

Camara, Dom Helder. *Church and Colonialism.* New York: Sheed & Ward, 1969. A collection of essays by the outstanding proponent of revolutionary nonviolence in Latin America; see especially chapter 10, "Violence —the Only Way?"

Derr, Thomas Sieger, *Ecology and Human Liberation.* Geneva, Switzerland: the WSCF Books, 1973. A theological critique of the use and abuse of our birthright.

Douglass, James. *The Non-Violent Cross.* New York: Macmillan, 1968. The theology of nonviolence and the nonviolent transformation of men. He makes a strong case for pacifism as the Christian position.

Edwards, George. *Jesus and the Politics of Violence.* New York: Harper & Row, 1972. A careful biblical study suggesting that Jesus was an apostle of nonviolent change and that his approach can be adopted by twentieth-century Christians.

Gutiérrez, Gustavo. *A Theology of Liberation.* Maryknoll,

N.Y.: Orbis Books, 1972. A political-sociological analysis and theological rationale for the movement from "development" to "liberation."

Hengel, Martin. *Victory Over Violence: Jesus and the Revolutionaries.* Philadelphia: Fortress Press, 1973. Deals with "political theology" and the possible use of violence in revolution. He argues that Jesus renounced the Zealots' use of violence, and demands nonviolent love.

International Documentation on the Contemporary Church, ed. *When All Else Fails: Christian Arguments on Violent Revolution.* Philadelphia: Pilgrim Press, 1970. The Christian's role in the midst of social and political revolution on a global scope. Special attention is paid to the Third World, especially Latin America.

Macquarrie, John. *The Concept of Peace.* New York: Harper & Row, 1973. Deals with peace as both technique and concept, from a philosophical and theological perspective.

Marty, Martin E., and Peerman, Dean G., eds. *New Theology No. 6.* New York: Macmillan, 1969. On revolution and nonrevolution, violence and nonviolence, peace and power, a useful introduction to many of the problems.

May, Rollo. *Power and Innocence: A Search For The Source of Violence.* New York: Norton, 1972. A psychological study that provides important background for the psychological chapter in the present book; particularly helpful on "the anatomy of violence."

Swomley, John. *Liberation Ethics.* New York: Macmillan, 1972. The role of violence in producing revolutionary change, written from a pacifist perspective and stressing the need for structural change throughout society.

Yoder, John. *The Politics of Jesus*. Grand Rapids: Eerdmans, 1972. A careful and well-documented treatment
of Jesus' teachings, the social message of the New
Testament, written from a pacifist perspective. He
argues that nonresisting love is the ethic of Jesus.

Contributors

Gerhard L. Belgum is Director of the Center for Theological Study, Thousand Oaks, California.

Otto Bremer is Campus Pastor, University of California-Santa Barbara, and Lecturer in Business Ethics, University of Southern California.

William Lesher is President of Pacific Lutheran Theological Seminary, Berkeley, California.

Sigurd Lokken is Campus Pastor, University of California-Berkeley, and Lutheran Pastor for Campus Ministries, San Francisco Metropolitan Area.

Charles P. Lutz is Director for Church in Community, Division for Life and Mission in the congregation, of the American Lutheran Church. He formerly served the Lutheran Council in the United States of America as Military Draft Specialist.

Ralph L. Moellering is Pastor for Special Ministries, Berkeley, California, for the Lutheran Church-Missouri Synod, and part-time Professor of History, University of California-Santa Cruz.

Gerald O. Pedersen is Pastor, Mount of Olives Lutheran Church, Mission Viejo, California. He formerly served as Campus Pastor, San Francisco State University, and as Chaplain, University of East Africa, Dar es Salaam, Tanzania.

Vernon L. Strempke is Professor of Pastoral Theology at the Pacific Lutheran Theological Seminary, Berkeley, California.